DANIEL ROSE, PH.D

AN EDUCATOR'S COMPANION

A GUIDE TO THE KOREN CHILDREN'S SIDDUR
ASHKENAZ

KOREN PUBLISHERS JERUSALEM

An Educator's Companion
A Guide to the Koren Children's Siddur
Nusaḥ Ashkenaz

First Edition © Koren Publishers Jerusalem Ltd. 2014

POB 4044, Jerusalem 91040, Israel
POB 8531, New Milford, CT 06776, USA
www.korenpub.com

Illustrations by Rinat Gilboa © Koren Publishers Jerusalem Ltd.
Koren Tanakh Font © 1962, 2013 Koren Publishers Jerusalem Ltd.
Koren Siddur Font and text design © 1981, 2013 Koren Publishers Jerusalem Ltd.

Large size, paperback, ISBN 978 965 301 682 8

Introduction to the Koren Magerman Educational Siddur Series

"Prayer is the language of the soul in conversation with God. It is the most intimate gesture of the religious life, and the most transformative." (Rabbi Jonathan Sacks)

These are the words with which Rabbi Sacks begins his introduction to the Koren Sacks Siddur. The act of praying can be transformative intellectually as well as spiritually and emotionally. To engage in the act of praying is to testify to the fundamentals of our faith: That the world was created by a benevolent God who participates in the history of the universe He created. There is purpose to our existence and destiny to our lives. But prayer can also be a crying out from deep within the soul. It is the aim of this siddur series to serve as a tool to encourage and facilitate our children's engagement in *tefilla* both cognitively and emotionally, leading to an overall spiritual development.

This Koren Magerman Educational Siddur Series is an exciting new project that signals a refreshing and innovative approach to *Tefilla* education in the school, home and synagogue. Each siddur in the series is appropriately designed for its developmental stage of the day-school journey, and beyond. With emphasis placed firmly on the critical foundations of Reflection, Connection, and Learning, this series of siddurim creates an impactful prayer experience that places God and the user at its center.

This first siddur in the series, the Koren Children's Siddur, will be developmentally appropriate for use in school, shul, and the home, for children in grades K–2 (5–7 years old). This siddur will be a bridge to a Koren Siddur for grades 3–5, which will in turn transition to a Koren Siddur for grades 6–8, and the Koren Ani Tefilla Siddur (grades 9–12). The Koren Children's Siddur combines stimulating and beautiful illustrations with thought-provoking educational components on each page to provide teachers and parents with an educational resource as much as a conventional siddur. The siddur is also accompanied by this Educator's Companion, a comprehensive guide for teachers and parents, to maximize the educational potential of this beginner's siddur.

The Educator's Companion complements the siddur as an educational resource, to provide support to the educator and parent in the form of a thorough explanation of every page of the siddur, and suggestions of how to use the siddur in a day-school or congregational context.

Acknowledgements

Many people contributed to both the siddur itself, and to this Educator's Companion and we would like to take this opportunity to express our thanks here. The siddur was extensively reviewed by the members of the Educational Editorial Board, namely Rabbi Boruch Sufrin, Rabbi Adam Englander, and Rabbi Dr. Jay Goldmintz. Their feedback was invaluable to the development of the siddur. The following early childhood education specialists also provided invaluable input and deserve much thanks: Wendy Kellner, Anna Hartman, Chayim Dimont, Hadassah Smolarcik, Desi Yishai, and Leah Summers. Special thanks to Rabbi Dr. Jay Goldmintz, Rachel Meghnagi, and Rabbi David Fuchs for reviewing this Educator's Companion, and sharing their insightful feedback and comments. Thanks also to Michal Britman and Tani Bayer at Koren for typesetting and graphics support.

The Educational Vision

When we consider the paths toward a relationship with God, we need not only consider the knowledge that will help us understand God but the skills that will help us interact with and access God too. We recognize that prophecy is a skill beyond most so we settle for the ability to read the siddur and to perform the mechanics of *tefilla*. We assume that regular performance of these actions will lead to emotional and spiritual connections with God. After all,

"אחרי הפעולות נמשכים הלבבות – The heart is drawn after action" (*Sefer HaḤinukh* mitzva 16). We expect that a child who reads his or her prayers regularly will have a meaningful spiritual experience as a result. Of course, many educators, parents, and children know this not to be entirely true. Indeed, even those who are adept at reading the *tefillot* and navigating the choreography throughout the siddur, still do not necessarily experience God with any greater sense of spirituality than those who struggle through the siddur. Thus, we are left with the question, if we accept the concept of אחרי הפעולות נמשכים הלבבות, then what are those actions that will lead to inspiration and connection?

An encounter with God requires preparation that amounts to building a relationship with Him. Without such a relationship, how can one expect to have deep meaningful conversations, sharing the most intimate details of one's life? How can one expect to experience God in prayer without preparing for such an encounter by building a relationship with God in other ways? We transact all the time with strangers – the checkout person at the store, for example. We want *tefilla*, though, to be more than a transactional experience for our children and thus aspire for them to have a relationship with God as a Father, as a King, and as something greater, in order for them to experience God in meaningful ways during *tefilla*. Engaging children in conversations about God, sharing with children the connectors and disconnectors that you experience related to God, bringing God into the mundane as well as the lofty will help children appreciate that which is transcendent and prepare them for encounters with God. Then, built on that relationship, prayer can become a heavenly experience. These are the types of actions that will lead to the emotional connection before and during *tefilla* – אחרי הפעולות נמשכים הלבבות.

So what, then, of the siddur itself? How can the siddur support this heavenly experience? The underlying assumption of this series of siddurim is that *tefilla* is more than a reading exercise, and the object of *tefilla* is not simply mastery of the *tefillot* themselves. Rather, God and the *mitpallel* are partners in the act of *tefilla*, together with the family, community, and others that comprise the world of the *mitpallel*. Unfortunately, too often in our schools, homes, and synagogues, the words of the siddur are the focus of *tefilla* as we pray. We focus on keeping our students' exactly on the right word, pronouncing the words perfectly, and following the mechanics and choreography of prayer. No doubt, these are important and we are not suggesting that reading is not a component of prayer education worthy of time in the curriculum. We would, in fact, urge schools to find ways outside of *tefilla* to have students practice reading the words of the siddur. That is, preparation for accuracy in reading the *tefillot* is important. However, this should not be the focus during *tefilla*. And, as we said earlier, such accuracy alone will likely not lead to experiencing God during *tefilla*.

The Koren Children's Siddur, and the series of siddurim that follow, highlight the child as an actor in prayer, asking questions and making statements that urge the child to think and engage with the world and the God that created it, directs it, and supports it daily.

It is important to note that we have purposefully chosen particular *tefillot*, guided by the centrality of those *tefillot* objectively, and also by their relevance to the daily lives of children. We have followed the guiding principle of "less is more" with regard to quantity of prayers, as the goal is to give the children a developmentally appropriate amount of text and keep the focus on the making of meaning. We appreciate those who question the omission of certain *tefillot* that their class currently recites or that a parent recalls fondly from their own upbringing. But we encourage you to consider whether the additional prayers you would include would detract from the focus we have articulated. With the goal of strengthening the spiritual connection in mind, we, along with our practitioner colleagues on the Educational Editorial Board of this series have concluded that a recalibration of *tefilla* education and the role of the siddur is necessary.

We all aspire for a relationship with God for ourselves and for our children. Rather than counting solely on the words of prayer to build a relationship with God, we believe a strengthened relationship can prepare us for and support us through prayer. This series of siddurim is a requisite tool for enabling this shift, as it empowers the student to go beyond the words to build on his or her relationship with God.

Dr. Scott Goldberg
Chairman, Koren Educational Editorial Board
Dr. Daniel Rose
Director of Educational Projects, Koren Publishers
Jerusalem
Adar I 5774 (February 2014)

The Koren Children's Siddur Explained

The Liturgical Text

One of the central educational goals of the Koren Magerman Educational Siddur Series is that the student, by progressing through the four developmentally appropriate siddurim, will graduate the program of *tefilla* education with the breadth and depth of *tefilla* skills and emotional and cognitive relationship to the liturgy necessary to feel total comfort and engagement with the adult siddur. Motivated by this goal, we have tried at every possible appropriate opportunity to create bridges between each of the siddurim, from the Koren Children's Siddur, to the adult Koren Siddur.

As much as possible, the structure of the adult Koren Siddur has been retained, with the Hebrew text of the *tefillot* on the left-hand page, and educational resources (see below) on the facing page (where the translation is found in the adult siddur). This aesthetic, together with the use of the Koren font and paragraph format-ting, will allow the student to be immediately famil-iar and at ease with the adult siddur whenever they encounter it. The dimensions of all the siddurim in the series also match those of the adult Koren Siddur for the same reason.

The font size varies depending on the amount of text on the page. In principle, the font size chosen is as large as possible without unduly compromising the other elements of the page such as the illustration and rubric (instructional sentence). This is essential for this first-stage siddur, allowing the siddur to func-tion as a resource for early-childhood Hebrew literacy. Those pages in the siddur that have a larger amount of text (and therefore a smaller font size) tend to contain those *tefillot* that are learnt through song rather than reading, such as *Adon Olam* and *Shema*, and so size of font is less critical.

Educational Components And Resources On The Page

On each page of the siddur several educational ele-ments have been built into the page, either for teachers to reference in the classroom as they would a textbook, or simply for the student to find engaging should their mind wander during the *tefilla*. If the student does find themselves losing focus, these resources func-tion as a constructive distraction for them. Better they should still be engaged in the siddur page than with other external distractions. Great thought has been put into each and every page to maximize the educa-tional potential of the siddur as a resource in school. No element of this siddur has been inserted for merely aesthetic purposes alone, but rather each is designed to be used as a resource for the educator.

The Illustrations

For each page of the siddur the illustrator was given a choice of several educational themes inspired by the text of the *tefilla* found on that page; these were based on the general meaning behind the prayer, or a specific line from the text, or a related educational objective. A guide to understanding each illustration and its educational potential is found in this Educator's Companion. If the illustration was inspired by or relates to a specific line of text from the liturgy, that line of the text appears in a color taken from the illustration, making a clear link in an aesthetically pleasing yet subtle way. This is not to overemphasize this line of the text or suggest it is more important or prominent in any way, but merely to draw attention to the thematic link between the illustration and the text of the *tefilla*.

The Navigation Bar

The Navigation Bar appears at the bottom of every left-hand page. This is a subtle navigational tool designed to familiarize the student with the structure of *Tefillat Shaharit*, enabling their awareness of where in the process of *tefilla* they are at any given point. The Navigation Bar illustrates the concept of ascent to the presence of God (while saying the *Shema* and *Amida*) and then descent back to the routine of everyday life.

The aesthetic of the Navigation Bar has been inspired by this idea of ascent/descent in *tefilla* as expressed by Rabbi Jonathan Sacks in his Introduction to the Koren Siddur.[1] Rabbi Sacks sees the structure of *tefilla* through the metaphor of Yaakov's ladder. Prayer is the ladder, and we are the angels, ascending to heaven and then descending back to earth. This reflects the structure of *tefilla* as creation-revelation-redemption. *Birkhot HaShahar* and *Pesukei DeZimra*, with the theme of creation, allow us to ascend to the summit of the ladder, and stand in the presence of God while we say the *Shema* and *Amida*.[2] From here prayer begins its descent as we turn to the theme of redemption with *Keriat*

HaTorah, *Ashrei* and *Aleinu*, allowing us to redeem our everyday lives by bringing the emotional-spiritual experience of *tefilla* (as experienced in the presence of God while at the summit of the ladder) into the routine of our everyday lives. We are now ready to reenter life and its challenges.

Each of the icons found on the Navigation Bar represents one of the eight identified sections of *Tefillat Shaharit*. The icon representing the current section of *tefilla* will be indicated by a stronger shade, while the other seven icons will be dimmed. The icons and meaning behind them are found here:

 הכנה לתפילה – Preparation for Tefilla (pre-*Birkhot HaShahar tefillot*) is represented by a character praying before getting out of bed.

 ברכות השחר – Morning Blessings are represented by the morning sun.

 פסוקי דזמרה – Verses of Praise (or Verses of Song) are represented by a musical note.

 קריאת שמע – The *Shema* is represented by a character lifting the hand to cover the eyes.

 עמידה – The *Amida* is represented by a character standing during this *tefilla*.

 קריאת התורה – The Reading of the Torah (or verses said when removing the *Sefer Torah* from the *Aron Kodesh*) is represented by a *Sefer Torah*.

 אבינו מלכנו – *Avinu Malkenu*, said on fast days and between Rosh HaShana and Yom Kippur, is represented by a *shofar*.

---

1. This is a well-known idea which was developed by the early kabbalists, and also succinctly expressed in the siddur of Rabbi Yaakov Emden.
2. It should be noted that in Rabbi Sacks' essay, the *Amida* alone is the pinnacle of the prayer experience, and should be at the apex of the ladder on its own. However, for aesthetic and logistical reasons we have placed the *Shema* and *Amida* together as the summit of the ascent of *Tefilla*. We believe that this is justifiable educationally as well; the *Shema*, being the ultimate declaration of faith and a *tefilla* of sufficient gravitas and intense emotion, can comfortably sit side by side with the experience of standing in front of God while praying the *Shemoneh Esreh*.

עלינו – *Aleinu* (and concluding *tefillot*) is represented by a bowing character.

The second section of the siddur that contains non-weekday morning prayers, such as the bedtime *Shema* and Shabbat *tefillot*, will have a different navigation bar containing the following four icons:

 ליל שבת – The Shabbat Evening *tefillot* are represented by an icon containing Shabbat candles.

 יום שבת – The remaining *tefillot* for Shabbat day are represented by an icon containing the traditional Shabbat items of a *Kiddush* cup and *ḥallot* (despite these also being relevant for Shabbat Evening).

 תפילה לשלום המדינה – The Prayer for the State of Israel is represented by an icon containing a *Magen David*.

 קריאת שמע על המיטה – The final page of our siddur is the bedtime *Shema*, which has its own icon that represents nighttime with a moon and stars.

Kavanot

Every page of the siddur (where space allows) has one or two thought elements to encourage the child to engage in the *tefilla* emotionally and cognitively. We have termed these "*Kavanot*," as they are designed to "direct" the child toward a particular idea from the *tefilla*, or line of thought, encouraging them toward a process of reflection, connection and learning.

The *kavanot* found on the page will often include a thought question, but could also take the form of a quote, statement, or a line of translation from the text of the *tefilla*. They are designed to lead the student on a thought process engaging in the text and the siddur in a cognitive and emotional way. In the Educator's Companion the teacher will be encouraged to use these questions and thoughts when appropriate, perhaps focusing on a different one each day. The teacher could use the question/thought as a trigger for a class discussion, or simply ask the children to reflect on the question/thought, as they say the *tefilla* or throughout their day (perhaps to be referenced later in the day in a different class).

When logistically possible, questions are contained in a "cloud" thought box, and statements/quotes in a speech bubble. This is a consistent theme contained throughout the siddur, and allows the child immediately to understand what they are encountering and what is expected of them (i.e., to answer a question or reflect on an idea). Statements that are quotes are always found in quotation marks. The source of the quote will only be found in this Educator's Companion, unless the quote is from Tanakh, in which case it is found in parentheses immediately after the quote. Sometimes, quotes are paraphrased in order to adapt the language to make it appropriate for this age group. In these cases, quotation marks are still used, as the essence of the quote remains.

Rubrics

On several pages a rubric (instructional sentence) is provided, aimed at aiding the student (or helping the teacher to aid the student) to understand the choreography of the *tefilla* service. A short instruction explaining what is required of the participant is found together with a visual instruction in the form of an icon.

The following icons have been incorporated into rubrics in the siddur:

 Boys say

 Girls say

 Netilat Yadayim (ritual hand washing)

 Hold the *tzitzit* (for *Barukh SheAmar* or for the *Shema*)

 Cover eyes for the first line of the *Shema*

Take three steps forward at the beginning of the *Amida* and three steps back at the end

   Amida bowing icons

 Tefillot that are said between Rosh HaShana and Yom Kippur, or on fast days

 Additional *tefilla* for unwell people in the *Amida*

   Special bowing for conclusion of the *Amida*

 Verses said before *Keriat HaTorah*

 The bedtime *Shema*

 Various *tefillot* that are traditionally sung on Shabbat

 A generic praying icon, most often used for *Amida*-related instructions

 Al HaNissim, said on Ḥanukka and Purim

 The blessing on lighting the Shabbat candles

 Bowing at specific times in certain *tefillot*

Page-by-Page Guide

This next section of the Educator's Companion will explore and explain each page spread from the siddur in detail, and provide ideas and strategies for the educator to best maximize the educational potential of each page. Each page of this guide will present the following resources in order to do this:

- The text of the *tefilla* translated (from the Koren Sacks Siddur) with educational themes from the text listed (for exploration independently from the other elements found on the page of the siddur)
- The illustration fully explained, together with suggested discussions that could emanate from it
- Ideas for using the *kavanot*

This will give the educator flexibility in how they wish to use the siddur in their own particular educational context. For example, the classroom teacher could choose to focus on one spread for a 5–10-minute period each day during the *tefilla* session over one week; one day on the meaning of the text, the next day on the illustration, a day on each *kavana*, and then a final day to summarize and reflect on everything the class has learned that week and their new understanding of the *tefilla*. Or perhaps the teacher wishes to abridge the *tefilla* one day a week, and dedicate 30 minutes to consider a *tefilla* using all the educational elements of the page at the same time. The congregational *tefilla* leader, with weekly programming opportunities, could choose to explore a different page in depth as part of the more extended time they have with the children, or may also wish to compare and contrast different spreads.

מודה אני
Modeh Ani

The Tefilla Text

Translation: *I thank You, living and eternal King, for giving me back my soul in mercy. Great is Your faithfulness.*

The text of this fundamental tefilla with which we begin our day has been reproduced in both the masculine and feminine to ensure that both girls and boys feel the same equal connection to the text, encouraging a personal connection to the words. This will also limit the confusion caused by including both genders within the same sentence, which this siddur avoids as much as possible.

The words מודה אני לפניך are highlighted in brown, anchoring them to the phrase "thank you" which is found in the upper *kavana*.

Educational Themes contained in the text:

- God as "King"/Kingship (מלכות)
- God as Creator of the world
- Gratitude
- Life is a gift from God
- Waking, renewal, creation.
- Gender specific relationships with God

The Illustration

In this first illustration of the siddur, our two main characters are encountered for the first time, the twins, Ellie and Dov. Here we see them in their bedroom first thing in the morning as they wake to a brand new day. The window gives us a glimpse of the world outside, with the bright blue sky of a new morning full of optimism and potential. The most striking aspect of the illustration educationally is the rays of sunshine shining through the window into the bedroom of our new friends. These rays represent the light and goodness of Hashem shining on His world as He returns the souls of His creations to them after the dark night. In fact, these rays could even be considered a manifestation of the souls of Ellie and Dov as they are returned to them by Hashem.

The Kavanot[3]

The Upper *Kavana: What do you want to say "thank you" for today?*

This is a reflection question, asking the child to reflect on what they have to be thankful for today. This *kavana* encourages the child to find themselves as the focus of the *tefilla* experience, and even become involved in authoring their own *tefillot* as they decide what they are saying thank you for. What do they have in their lives that they are thankful for? The educator should encourage them to recognize the blessings they have and then to be thankful for them. The final step is then to decide who to thank. God is not necessarily the only correct answer, and this in itself could be an appropriate discussion to be facilitated. Where do blessings come from? Do we create our own blessings from our own hard work or do they come from Hashem? Or is it perhaps a partnership? These questions encourage connection building to God and also the child's parents and family.

The beauty of this question is also that it can be asked every day, with a different answer given each time.

This approach, repeated exploration of this question, in itself has educational value.

The Lower *Kavana: "We thank Hashem for life itself. Life is a gift from Hashem."*

This is a paraphrased quote from the commentary of Rabbi Jonathan Sacks in the Koren Sacks Siddur. This *kavana* asks the children to consider life itself as a gift not to be taken for granted. Educators could choose to discuss this quote, pursuing any of the following directions:

- Who is responsible for our birth and existence?
- Why is saying "thank you" important?
- If we have a difficult life should we still say "thank you"?
- Did Hashem give us the gift of life once at our birth or does He continually give us this gift every day?
- Why is this the first *tefilla* we say in the morning and, in fact, the first words we say the moment we wake up?

---

3. The terms "Upper Kavana" and "Lower Kavana" have been chosen for practical reasons, to indicate which *kavana* is being referred to. No deeper spiritual qualification is being made.

עַל נְטִילַת יָדַיִם
The Blessing on Washing Hands

The Tefilla Text

Translation: *Blessed are You, LORD our God, King of the Universe, who has made us holy through His commandments, and has commanded us about washing hands.*

The word "יָדַיִם" in the blessing is highlighted in light brown, as is the word "hands" in the *kavana*, linking both words together and to Ellie's hands (which are a similar color).

Educational Themes contained in the text:

- The choreography of this mitzva
- Hands = action/behavior
- Dedication of something for holiness
- נטל = taking, elevating, for higher moral purpose

The Illustration

This illustration is primarily instructional in nature, and has Ellie taking the special "*natla*" cup dedicated for the ritual washing of hands and filling it with water from the running faucet in order to fulfill this mitzva. The halakhic aspects of the cup (for example the minimum amount of water necessary to perform this ritual is 86cc according to the more lenient approach; the mouth of the vessel must have a continuous rim; etc.) could be explored from the illustration, and the association between this mitzva and the ritual of the *Kohanim* in the *Beit HaMikdash*, who also washed their hands with a vessel to purify them, could also be explored. This line of thought introduces the children to the concepts of holiness and purity, and although both are difficult and abstract concepts for this developmental stage, the concepts could still be discussed at an introductory level. Rabbi S.R. Hirsch also makes the connection between this mitzva and the Kohanim in the *Beit HaMikdash*, and speaks about the "dedication" of our hands and our bodies to holiness. He uses the root נ-ט-ל as the source for this idea – to elevate ones hands.

While the section of floor that Ellie is standing on looks like it is appropriate for a bathroom setting, the coloring and pattern of the rest of the illustration is more abstract and has a more spiritual feel to it, while also reflecting the shapes and colors of water. Perhaps this could be a reflection of the spiritual feelings in Ellie's mind while she performs the first mitzva of the day with water.

The Kavanot

The Upper *Kavana*: *What else are you going to do with your hands today?*

This is a reflection question, asking the child to reflect on their day ahead and on how they are going to interact with their world during that time. Hands represent action and behavior, one way that we interact and create things in this world. It is interesting to note that the blessing for this Mitzva does not focus on washing or water, but rather places emphasis and focus on hands. This kavana asks the child to consider what potential they have to achieve with their hands and implicitly asks them to consider making sure they use them for "holy" purposes. An appropriate follow up question would be "how can we dedicate our hands to holy purposes"? and "what would Hashem want us to use our hands for"?

The Lower *Kavana*: *Water sometimes moves and changes, and is sometimes still. When will you move and when will you be still today?*

This is a reflection question, asking the child to consider the properties of water and how water may be similar to us. Water is constantly on the move, changing and adapting, busily going about achieving its goals. However, under the appropriate circumstances, water can also be very still and quiet. Still waters run deep. This question asks the child to consider when in their day will they be like the first property of water, and when more like the latter property. The implied message is that both modes of existence and being are appropriate in their correct time. The educator may also like to use this opportunity to explore other educational values inherent in water, such as water as life-giving as we start our day anew with this ritual (Rashba) or the comparison of water to the Torah (*Bava Kama* 82a). This may also provide an opportunity to be creative and use actual water as a visual aid for this educational moment.

אשר יצר
Asher Yatzar

"Judaism sees the doctor as Hashem's messenger."

The Tefilla Text

Translation: *Blessed are You, LORD our God, King of the Universe, who formed man in wisdom and created in him many orifices and cavities. It is revealed and known before the throne of Your glory that were one of them to be ruptured or blocked, it would be impossible to survive and stand before You. Blessed are You, LORD, Healer of all flesh who does wondrous deeds.*

Educational Themes contained in the text:

- The miracle of life/the human body
- The holiness of the human body as well as the soul
- God as the Creator of the world and of man
- Healing and God as Healer
- The fragility of human life

The Illustration

The illustration is largely instructional, depicting Ellie saying this special blessing having left the bathroom. This provides an educational opportunity to consider the halakhic requirements of this blessing, including the divergent opinions as to whether some blessings should be said at home as the relevant acts are performed, or whether they should be said in the synagogue at the beginning of *Shaḥarit*. Also the notion that we do not mention the name of Hashem in a place that is not befitting, such as a bathroom, could be discussed here (hence Ellie is seen outside the bathroom rather than inside it), as well as the special nature of holy articles such as the siddur, which should not be taken into the bathroom. Here Ellie is saying the blessing having just left the bathroom (notice the wash basin from the previous page spread can be seen through the bathroom door) and this would be a good time to mention that this is not a *tefilla*, but rather a blessing said throughout the day.

The Kavanot

The Upper *Kavana*: *What do you think is the most important part of your body? Why?*

This question asks the child to reflect on the wondrous and intricate nature of the human body and the importance of each and every limb and organ. The ultimate message of this blessing is that life without even one of these would be difficult if not impossible. Rather than focusing on the negative (how terrible it would be to not have a particular limb or organ), this *kavana* asks the child to reflect on how important each part of their body is, and choose which they think is the most important. This presents the educator with a creative opportunity to discuss this, such as having an auction (children have limited funds to buy the body parts they value the most, and then justify their choice at the end), or a balloon debate (children playing the role of given body parts give an argument why they should remain in the sinking hot air balloon) to decide.

The Lower *Kavana*: *"Judaism sees the doctor as Hashem's messenger."*

This is a paraphrased quote from J. David Bleich in his book *Judaism and Healing* (although it can be considered a generally accepted normative idea in Jewish thought). This *kavana* asks the child to consider how Hashem provides and protects for us, and to explore the partnership we have with Him in our lives to look after ourselves and the world. Additional concepts that can be discussed as an outgrowth of this could be the injunction to not rely on miracles, Hashem as the source of mankind's inspiration and knowledge, Divine Providence and God's role in the world and our lives, supernatural and natural miracles. The link between this *kavana* and the text of the blessing is the human body. While in this blessing we marvel at its beauty, intricacies, and design, and connect and show gratitude to its Creator by reciting it, we are also aware of our responsibility to look after it, and that it is a religious imperative to do that. Our bodies should be considered a gift from Hashem, which is actually on loan. We have a moral responsibility to look after it until He chooses to take it back.

א-לוהי נשמה
Elohai Neshama

¹ אֱלֹהַי

² נְשָׁמָה שֶׁנָּתַתָּ בִּי טְהוֹרָה הִיא.

³ אַתָּה בְרָאתָהּ, אַתָּה יְצַרְתָּהּ

⁴ אַתָּה נְפַחְתָּהּ בִּי וְאַתָּה מְשַׁמְּרָהּ בְּקִרְבִּי

⁵ וְאַתָּה עָתִיד לִטְּלָהּ מִמֶּנִּי

⁶ וּלְהַחֲזִירָהּ בִּי לֶעָתִיד לָבוֹא.

⁷ כָּל זְמַן שֶׁהַנְּשָׁמָה בְקִרְבִּי

⁸ 🧍‍♀️ מוֹדָה 🧍 מוֹדֶה

⁹ אֲנִי לְפָנֶיךָ

¹⁰ יהוה אֱלֹהַי וֵאלֹהֵי אֲבוֹתַי

¹¹ רִבּוֹן כָּל הַמַּעֲשִׂים, אֲדוֹן כָּל הַנְּשָׁמוֹת.

¹² בָּרוּךְ אַתָּה יהוה

¹³ הַמַּחֲזִיר נְשָׁמוֹת לִפְגָרִים מֵתִים.

What makes people different from animals?

"And Hashem breathed into man's nose the soul of life, and man became a living being" (*Bereshit* 2:7).

The Tefilla Text

Translation: *My God, the soul You placed within me is pure. You created it, You formed it, You breathed it into me, and You guard it while it is within me. One day You will take it from me, and restore it to me in the time to come. As long as the soul is within me, I will thank You,* LORD *my God and God of my ancestors, Master of all works,* LORD *of all souls. Blessed are You,* LORD, *who restores souls to lifeless bodies.*

The word נשמה is highlighted in brown, anchoring it to the upper *kavana*. The word נפחתה is highlighted in green, anchoring it to the lower *kavana*.

Inside the *tefilla*, the word מודה is found in the masculine and feminine, indicated by the boy and girl icons.

Educational Themes contained in the text:

• The soul and its divine source

- The duality of man as both a physical and spiritual being
- השגחה פרטית – Divine Providence
- Gratitude
- God as Creator of the world, both physical and spiritual

- Our soul is pure and we have free choice to lead it to be good or bad
- Mankind is inherently good (implied by the fact that the soul Hashem has given us is "pure")

The Illustration

The illustration depicts a creation scene, with several elements mentioned in the creation story in the Torah, such as the land and sea, trees and vegetation, fish and animals. The scene is full of life with the colors green and blue being primary. However, the focus of the illustration, and its connection to this *tefilla*, is the presence of the first of mankind – Adam and Eve. This encourages the viewer to consider the physical creation of man. Adam and Eve are partially obscured by the vegetation, mainly to avoid the tricky decision of how to clothe them. However this also draws attention to their faces (which some might say is the physical manifestation of the soul). This is the connection between the *tefilla* and the illustration. This *tefilla*, describing the creation of our soul and expressing gratitude to Hashem for returning it each morning, is a companion to the previous blessing אשר יצר, which describes our physical bodies. The creation scene is where both of these aspects of our existence were created.

The Kavanot

The Upper *Kavana*: *What makes people different from animals?*

This *kavana* asks the child to reflect on what it means to be a human being. It is anchored to the word נשמה in the text, as this is one of the possible answers to the question. The soul that Hashem gave us, that we mention and show gratitude for in this *tefilla*, is not given to any of the animals. Other possible answers could include the power of speech, abstract thought, freewill, the ability to distinguish between right and wrong/good and evil, and the capability to have a relationship with God. Perhaps all of these can be directly linked to the soul that man has that is absent in all other living creatures. It is this soul that is returned to us each morning, and that we thank Hashem for in this *tefilla*. Only man is described as being created "in the image of God" and it is this soul that makes him unique.

The Lower *Kavana*: *"And Hashem breathed into man's nose the soul of life and man became a living being"* (Bereshit 2:7).

This quote from the Torah describes the moment that Adam received the soul that is mentioned in this *tefilla*. This is the same soul that each of the children reading this *kavana* has received, and this *kavana* asks them to reflect on that, and what it might mean for their lives. Many questions and ideas can be generated from this verse, each justifying a discussion on its own.

- Why does the verse use the word נפחת which we translate as "breathe" as the action of Hashem placing this soul into Adam's body? Does Hashem have a nose or mouth in order to be able to "breathe" something?
- Why is it Adam's nose that receives his soul? What do we breathe through our noses? Could this be teaching something about the nature of the soul (what are the similarities between air and the soul?)
- What does the term "the soul of life" mean? Can one live without a soul? Who or what does live without a soul and what is their life like?
- If only at this point did man become a "living being," then what was he before this point? And what is he after the soul departs?

ציצית
Tzitzit

The Tefilla Text

Translation: *Blessed are You, LORD our God, King of the Universe, who has made us holy through His commandments, and has commanded us about the command of tasseled garments.*

The word צִיצִית from the blessing is highlighted in green and thereby anchored to the upper *kavana*, which is a quote exploring *tzitzit* as a visual reminder of mitzvot.

Educational Themes contained in the text:

- Tzitzit as a visual reminder/signpost
- The concept of Mitzva
- God as Ruler of the world
- Mitzvot as a source of holiness
- Jewish clothing

The Illustration

This illustration is largely instructional. Here we find Dov in the bedroom again next to his bed, as he gets dressed and ready for school. He holds his *tzitzit* out as he makes the blessing. Again, there are those that say this blessing immediately upon donning the *tallit katan* as Dov is, and those that would wait until they are praying from the siddur. While there is no halakhic obligation to hold the *tzitzit* when one says the bless-ing, this is something that young children are asked to do in a school setting for educational purposes, and functions as a way of emphasizing the ritual in the illustration. The lower *kavana*, which presents the famous *gematria* (numerical value) of the word ציצית, has been designed to look like a height chart on Dov and Ellie's wall.

The Kavanot

The Upper *Kavana*: "ציצית *are a reminder to us. We tie them to our clothes just as one might tie a string around his finger or belt to remember something."*

This is a paraphrased quote from Rabbi Aryeh Kaplan in his book *Tzitzit: A Thread of Light*. The language has been slightly modified to allow it to be more readily understood by this age group. The *kavana* encourages the child to understand the famous approach to the explanation behind the ritual of *tzitzit* – that it is a visual reminder for us. While tying a string around one's finger may not be a contemporary way to remind oneself of something important, the educator could ask the children to consider ways today that we do remind ourselves of things (e.g., writing ourselves a note, sending oneself an email, setting an alarm, writing an entry in a calendar, asking a friend or parent to remind us, etc.).

The question to be considered here is what is Hashem asking us to remember while we wear *tzitzit*? Possibly the most common way to answer this is Rashi's well-known approach presented in the lower *kavana*, that *tzitzit* remind us of all the mitzvot in the Torah, and the two *kavanot* on this page can work in tandem. However, there are other broader and more general answers to this question that are equally legitimate such as "the Torah," "being good," "Hashem," etc. The children can be asked what they think of when they see or wear *tzitzit*, and the discussion can emanate from there. An interesting but more abstract line of discussion could also be why we need signs and reminders in our life in general. The educator could introduce other signs from the world of the child (either by mentioning them or, more creatively, by bringing them into class, asking the children to create signs, or playing a game with them), including signs in school, traffic signs, advertising signs, warning signs in various contexts, etc., and follow up by exploring with the children why Hashem may want to provide us with a sign to remind us of His mitzvot/Torah.

The Lower *Kavana*:

ת י צ י צ

400 + 10 + 90 + 10 + 90 + 8 strings + 5 knots = ?

This well-known idea, that the mitzva of *tzitzit* should be considered a visual reminder of all the other mitzvot, comes from a Rashi on Bemidbar 15:39, where the numerical value of the word ציצית is given (צ = 90; י = 10; and ת = 400). This all comes to 600. Add to this the 8 strings (4 strings doubled over to form 8) and the 5 knots required to tie them all together, and it comes to 613, the number of mitzvot in the Torah. This simple arithmetic could be used creatively by the educator to explain this concept to the children. The concept of 613 mitzvot may be new to children of this age, and so the educator may also wish to explore that.

ברכות התורה 1
Blessings over the Torah 1

The Tefilla Text

Translation: *Blessed are You, LORD our God, King of the Universe, who has made us holy through His commandments, and has commanded us to engage in study of the words of Torah.*

Please, LORD our God, make the words of Your Torah sweet in our mouths and in the mouths of Your people, the house of Israel, so that we, our descendants (and their descendants) and the descendants of Your people, the house of Israel, may all know Your name and study Your Torah for its own sake. Blessed are You, LORD, who teaches Torah to His people Israel.

Educational Themes contained in the text:

- A blessing for learning Torah means it is a mitzva – divine command/spiritual experience (and not just an intellectual/educational act)
- The text of the blessing is to "engage in the words of the Torah" rather than merely "study" them.
- We pray that the Torah will be "sweet" in our mouths (as spiritual nourishment just like sweet food is physical nourishment)
- We pray that we will be successful in teaching it (and passing our enthusiasm) to our children

- Hashem is the source of the Torah, and He teaches it to us personally

- Learning Torah "for its own sake/לשמה"

The Illustration

In this illustration we have Ellie and Dov learning Torah from their own *sefarim*. While the Torah they learn is the very same Torah found in the synagogue and *Beit Midrash* (seen in the distance) the children have their own special connection and intimacy to it. In fact, the Torah has left the *Beit Midrash* and is central to their lives. The path that they sit on represents the אורך חיים/דרך and that the Torah must have relevance to our everyday lives, rather than remain in the distant synagogue or study hall. Perhaps this also reminds us that the study of Torah is not merely an intellectual activity, but must lead to action, and this is also reflected in the language of the blessing, "to engage in the words of Torah" rather than to merely study them.

The old study hall in the distance, surrounded by trees (עץ חיים as the Torah is referred to in *Mishlei* 3:18 – see the following page spread where this is more fully explored), could also represent the Torah of ancient times, and the path forms the link between then and now. The Torah the children hold is the very same Torah from ancient times, in the hands of the children who represent future generations. This Torah is as relevant today as it ever was, and the path represents an unbroken chain of heritage and tradition from ancient times, throughout Jewish history, until today and beyond to the future. The path, traversing green lush hills and yellow barren hills, shows us how the Torah has been ever-present throughout the ups and downs of Jewish history, and has proven to be eternal, just as the people that adhere to it.

The Kavanot

The Upper *Kavana*: *Why do we make a ברכה on learning Torah?*

This *kavana* asks the children to reflect on the nature of the mitzva to learn Torah as expressed in its blessings. Many subjects are learned in school, and we can find many varied reasons to learn them. But we only make a blessing on one of them. *Limmud Torah* is a mitzva, and divine injunction, commanded by Hashem, and therefore we make a blessing on performing this mitzva, just as we do for any other mitzva (this blessing is therefore a ברכת מצוה). There are many reasons why learning Torah would be a good idea (you may like to ask the children what they might be), but the ultimate reason we do it is because Hashem commanded us to. The educator may also wish to think slightly more creatively to answer this question (or perhaps one of the children will provide the answer) that this blessing is actually a ברכת נהנין made before partaking of something from which one gains enjoyment, such as food or fragrance. Learning Torah is an enjoyable experience, and the Torah is a gift from Hashem, and we therefore must make a blessing to thank Him, just as we do in other cases of enjoyment. This idea is also found in Rabbi J.B. Soloveitchik's approach to these blessings.

The Lower *Kavana*: *If praying is talking to Hashem, then learning Torah is listening to Hashem!*

This *kavana* asks the child to see *tefilla* and *Limmud Torah* as the two sides of their connection to Hashem. The *kavana* is based on a comment made by Rabbi Jonathan Sacks in his commentary on the *Shema* in the Koren Sacks Siddur. The full quote is: "In prayer, we speak to God. In the *Shema*, God, through the Torah, speaks to us." This creates for us the wonderful idea that *tefilla* is actually a dialogue. We speak to Hashem, and through His Torah, He speaks to us in return, and we must listen (hence "שמע"!). Perhaps this is why the compilers of our siddur made sure to place so many quotes from the Torah (including Tanakh), and why the *Shema* is central to our *tefilla* service. This also concretizes for the children the concept of *Torah min hashamayim* – the words we have in front of us literally came from the mouth of Hashem. That is what we are saying when we make a blessing on the mitzva of learning Torah.

ברכות התורה 2
Blessings over the Torah 2

What does it mean that the Torah is our "heritage"?

Hashem said to Avraham, "Through you, all the families of the world will be blessed" (*Bereshit* 12:3).

בָּרוּךְ אַתָּה יהוה ¹
אֱלֹהֵינוּ מֶלֶךְ הָעוֹלָם ²
אֲשֶׁר בָּחַר בָּנוּ מִכָּל הָעַמִּים ³
וְנָתַן לָנוּ אֶת תּוֹרָתוֹ. ⁴
בָּרוּךְ אַתָּה יהוה נוֹתֵן הַתּוֹרָה. ⁵

יְבָרֶכְךָ יהוה וְיִשְׁמְרֶךָ: ⁶
יָאֵר יהוה פָּנָיו אֵלֶיךָ וִיחֻנֶּךָּ: ⁷
יִשָּׂא יהוה פָּנָיו אֵלֶיךָ וְיָשֵׂם לְךָ שָׁלוֹם: ⁸

תּוֹרָה צִוָּה־לָנוּ מֹשֶׁה ⁹
מוֹרָשָׁה קְהִלַּת יַעֲקֹב: ¹⁰

The Tefilla Text

Translation: *Blessed are You,* LORD *our God, King of the Universe, who has chosen us from all the peoples and given us His Torah. Blessed are You,* LORD, *Giver of the Torah.*

May the LORD *bless you and protect you. May the* LORD *make His face shine on you and be gracious to you. May the* LORD *turn His face toward you and grant you peace.* (*Bemidbar* 6:24–26)

The Torah Moses commanded us is the heritage of the congregation of Jacob. (*Devarim* 33:4)

The words "אשר בחר בנו מכל העמים ונתן לנו את תורתו" are highlighted in brown to connect to the lower *kavana*, and the words "תורה צוה לנו משה מורשה קהלת יעקב" are highlighted in green to connect to the upper *kavana*.

Educational Themes contained in the text:

• We are "chosen" to be the only nation to receive the Torah, and with this comes the responsibility of being an "*Am Segula*"

- *Limmud Torah* is our gateway to understanding the ways of God
- Torah is *min hashamayim*
- Torah is "commanded" by Hashem (i.e., it is an imperative/instruction)

- The Torah that Moshe received, the same one we learn today, represents an unbroken tradition/heritage throughout the generations and our history

The Illustration

This illustration finds Dov and Ellie engaged in the mitzva of learning Torah. Dov is learning from his *sefer*, but Ellie is looking at the abstract expression of the Torah in the form of a tree, with the letters of the *Sefer Torah* floating from it. The Torah is described as עץ חיים (Tree of Life) in *Mishlei* (3:18), and here we have this represented by the letters from the Torah ascending to heaven from the tree. The educator may wish to consider with his/her students why the Torah is compared to a living tree. Possible directions to consider include the sustenance and nutrition that a tree can give, as well as the protection in the form of shade. A tree also provides for us the imagery of deep roots, and development and growth over generations, all of which are appropriate and relevant concepts to relate to the Torah.

The letters ascending from the tree toward heaven in this illustration remind us of the story in the Gemara (*Avoda Zara* 18a) of the martyrdom of Rabbi Ḥanan ben Teradyon, who was burned alive by the Roman authorities while wrapped in the parchment of a *Sefer Torah*. When his students asked him what he saw he replied that while the parchment was burning the letters were flying toward heaven. While it may be felt that this story is inappropriate for this age, the imagery and message of this story is a beautiful one that is expressed in our illustration and can be shared with children of this age. The words of the Torah begin their journey in heaven, and return to heaven, whether through trauma and disaster or through the voices of children learning them.

Finally, we also have the inspiring message that Torah learning and closeness to Hashem can come from *sefarim* and nature alike. While Dov is learning from his *sefer*, Ellie is looking at nature. In fact it seems almost as if Ellie is impacting Dov's learning from his *sefer* by pointing to the tree, and Dov is helping Ellie to understand what she is seeing from the wisdom in his *sefer*. This idea is clearly Maimonidean, as found in his introduction to the *Guide for the Perplexed*:

The Almighty, desiring to lead us to perfection, and to improve the state of our society, revealed to us His laws which are to regulate our actions. These laws... presuppose an advanced state of intellectual culture. We must first... have knowledge of metaphysics. But this discipline can only be approached after the study of physics... Therefore, the Almighty commenced Scripture with the descriptions of creation, that is, with physical science.

Our illustration is also reminiscent in a visual way of the Mishna in *Avot* (3:9):

Rabbi Jacob said: One who is reviewing his Torah study while walking on the way, and interrupts his study to say, "What a beautiful tree" or "What a beautiful field," is regarded by Scripture as if he had endangered his soul.

According to Rav A.I. HaKohen Kook the key word to understanding this mishna is the word "interrupts." When one looks at nature and sees this as an interruption to one's Torah learning, as something separate and spiritually inferior and less holy, then, according to the mishna, one incurs the ultimate penalty. Rather we should see the exploration and appreciation of God's world as a parallel and complimentary path to understanding and loving God. Clearly Ellie and Dov learn this mishna with the help of Rav Kook, as they see their Torah learning in nature, and nature in their Torah learning.

The Kavanot

The Upper *Kavana*: *What does it mean that the* תורה *is our "heritage"?*

This *kavana* asks the children to connect to the ancient chain of tradition that the Torah represents from their ancestors until today. It is anchored to the verse "תורה צוה לנו משה," a verse that will most likely be familiar to the children, especially through the popular tune that accompanies it. While the word "heritage" is not one that young children of this age will be familiar with, the concept is not strange to them at all. Heritage is something inherited at birth, whether possessions, characteristics, or status. While this is an appropriate definition for our context and applicable to the Torah, the secondary definition of the word is even more so. That is, something transmitted from the past and handed down as tradition. This *kavana* asks the child to connect to the 4000-year-old unbroken chain of tradition, from his or her ancestors, through grandparents and parents, to the child themselves today. That is the Torah that Dov and Ellie are holding on to in the illustration, and the book they hold in their hand today in the form of their siddur.

The Lower *Kavana*: *Hashem said to Avraham, "Through you, all the families of the world will be blessed" (Bereshit 12:3).*

This *kavana*, anchored to the words "אשר בחר בנו מכל העמים ונתן לנו את תורתו," asks the child to connect to the concept of chosenness, as found in the blessing for learning Torah. The blessing suggests that we have been chosen as a nation to receive the Torah. The verse from *Bereshit* suggests that Avraham has been chosen to be a blessing to all the families of the world. This blessing together with this verse, can present to us a broad concept of national election. We have been chosen to accept the Torah, and through fulfilling the precepts contained in the Torah, we can become a blessing to the world. The Jewish People can do this by behaving as a model nation, based on Torah values. In the words of Rabbi Jonathan Sacks (*To Heal a Fractured World*):

God asks one individual – eventually a family, a tribe, a collection of tribes, a nation – to serve as an exemplary role model, to be as it were a living case-study in what it is to live closely and continuously in the presence of God.

מה טבו
Ma Tovu

The Tefilla Text

Translation: *How goodly are your tents, Jacob, your dwelling places, Israel. As for me, in Your great loving-kindness, I will come into Your House. I will bow down to Your holy Temple in awe of You. LORD, I love the habitation of Your House, the place where Your glory dwells. As for me, I will bow in worship; I will bend the knee before the LORD my Maker. As for me, may my prayer come to You, LORD, at* a time of favor. *God, in Your great loving-kindness, answer me with Your faithful salvation.*

The words "אהליך יעקב משכנתיך ישראל" are highlighted in green to anchor them to the illustration, specifically the large tent, as well as both *kavanot*, which are both exploring the concept of Jewish structures/homes.

Educational Themes contained in the text:

- Tents = tents of learning (*Beit Midrash*)

- Tents = Jewish homes (which should also function as a *Beit Midrash* and *Beit Kenesset*)
- What makes your home a Jewish home?
- Parallel to our tent is God's tent = *Beit HaMikdash*

The Illustration

This illustration asks the children to reflect on the Jewish values that are expressed in Jewish buildings. It has our two characters traveling back in time (or perhaps they are the ancestors of Dov and Ellie who looked similar to them) and encountering Avraham (or perhaps any other biblical character) performing the mitzva of הכנסת אורחים (welcoming guests). The words of *Ma Tovu* come from the biblical story of Balak, and so the scene in the background of the illustration is reminiscent of a desert encampment, during the period when the Children of Israel were traveling from Egypt to the Land of Israel.

The illustration asks the child to explore the concept of a Jewish home. What does it mean that Jewish homes (tents and dwellings) are "goodly"? This question can be posed to the children using this illustration and is also related and connected to the upper *kavana*, "What makes a building Jewish?" The illustration suggests the answer is that a Jewish home is open to guests and strangers, a home in which the mitzva of הכנסת אורחים is central. Presenting the children in the illustration as visually like Dov and Ellie, but in a biblical context with biblical garb, suggests a continuity from the times of Tanakh until today, in terms of history, values, tradition and peoplehood.

The Kavanot

The Upper *Kavana*: *What makes a building "Jewish"?*

This *kavana*, anchored to the text "אהליך יעקב משכנ־תיך ישראל," asks the child to reflect on the nature of the Jewish home and community, and perhaps their place within it. There are many directions in which the discussion could go once this question is posed to the children. Is a building considered Jewish from its external structure, what is contained inside it, or from the behavior of the people that frequent it? The answer can be all three. A building that has been designed with Torah values – such as *Kavod HaBeriot*, protecting the environment – in mind can be considered a "Jewish building." Practically speaking this could include disability access features, energy efficiency, resource conservation or recycling. Or a "Jewish Building" could be one that contains articles of Jewish importance, such as ritual objects, *mezuzot* on every door, books of Jewish knowledge, or a kosher kitchen. But the most profound definition of a "Jewish Building" is one in

which the people who frequent the building act in a "Jewish way," performing mitzvot, and embodying Jewish values, such as הכנסת אורחים.

The Lower *Kavana*: "*And they will make a* משכן *for Me so that I may live among them*" (*Shemot 25:8*).

This kavana consists of the verse from the Torah instructing the Children of Israel in the desert to construct a tabernacle for God to dwell within. Placing this verse on this page asks the children to consider the similarities between our own "Jewish buildings" and the building created to contain the Divine Presence. What are the similarities between our homes and the *Beit HaMikdash*? Questions that may follow from this discussion include why does God need a dwelling place or is it that we need a place where we can consider ourselves "visiting" Him? Where do we go today to "visit" God? And what do we do when we get there?

אדון עולם
Adon Olam

The Tefilla Text

Translation: LORD *of the universe, who reigned before the birth of any thing – When by His will all things were made then was His name proclaimed King. And when all things shall cease to be He alone will reign in awe. He was, He is, and He shall be glorious for evermore. He is One, there is none else, alone, unique, beyond compare; Without beginning, without end, His might, His rule are everywhere. He is my God; my Redeemer lives. He is the Rock on whom I rely – My banner and my safe retreat, my cup, my portion when I cry. Into His hand my soul I* place, when I awake and when I sleep. The LORD is with me, I shall not fear; body and soul from harm will He keep.

The word "מֶלֶךְ" in the third line of the text is highlighted in light brown, and anchored to the word "King" in the upper *kavana*. The words of the penultimate line in the text are highlighted in green and anchored to the illustration in the form of the moon, representing Hashem's protection of Dov while he sleeps. The words of the last line of the text of the *tefilla* are highlighted in light brown and anchored to the lower *kavana* which is an adapted translation.

Educational Themes contained in the text:

- God as "King"
- God as Creator of the world
- God of the universe vs. Personal God
- God of History – He is infinite, pre-dates history, but is involved in the history of the universe, world, Jewish people, and our own history
- God protects me (my body and soul) when I sleep and when I wake up

The Illustration

This illustration asks the child to connect to Hashem as a King-Protector. The theme of the illustration is God's protection of our soul when we are asleep and when we are awake, and the child is asked to reflect on this aspect of their relationship with Hashem. In this way, the illustration complements the lower *kavana* which explores further the concept of God's protection as expressed in the translation of the last two lines of the text. The line of the text from which this concept is taken (בְּיָדוֹ אַפְקִיד רוּחִי. בְּעֵת אִישָׁן וְאָעִירָה) is highlighted in green, and is anchored to the color of the moon on which Dov is sleeping. We can see Dov sleeping safely and soundly in the comforting knowledge that Hashem is looking after him. In the bottom left-hand corner we have a waking Dov, alert and alive and ready to face the new day, aware of and rejoicing in the love and protection of Hashem.

The rays of light that emanate from the top left-hand corner of the page also represent God's protection (they are rays of light that deliberately do not emanate from the sun, and are barely perceptible, yet clearly a part of the image and the life of Dov in the illustration). The sun and the moon represent night and day, sleeping and waking, darkness and light. And throughout it all we can be assured that God is with us and protecting us. The musical notes that form the texture of the ground on the right-hand page remind us of the important role of music and song in our *tefilla*, and especially in this *tefilla*. *Adon Olam* may have more tunes associated with it than any other *tefilla* in the siddur.

The Kavanot

The Upper *Kavana*: *In what ways is Hashem like a King?*

The upper *kavana* asks the child to reflect on the theme of Kingship in the *tefilla*, designed to encourage the student to try and relate to God as a King. They are asked to do this by first clarifying for themselves what role a king plays in the lives of regular people, and how that may help us to understand and relate to God and the role He plays in our lives. Just as a king (or president) has power over our lives, as well as a responsibility to protect and provide for his subjects, so too, does Hashem. Just as we have a responsibility to show loyalty and respect to a king, so too to Hashem.

The Lower *Kavana*: *"Hashem will look after my soul and my body. Hashem is with me, I will not be afraid!"*

This quote is an adapted translation of the last line of the *tefilla*. This was chosen because it summarizes a central theme to the *tefilla*, and is one to which the child can relate, and may be inspired by. The teacher could simply ask the students to spend a moment reflecting on this line in silence, and then continue with the *tefilla*, or use this as a trigger to begin a discussion on fear in the lives of the students, and how faith in God can help navigate a world that is often scary. This translated line from the *tefilla* can also be related to the upper *kavana* as well as to the message of the illustration.

יגדל
Yigdal

25 24

יִגְדַּל

אֱלֹהִים חַי וְיִשְׁתַּבַּח

נִמְצָא וְאֵין עֵת אֶל מְצִיאוּתוֹ.

אֶחָד וְאֵין יָחִיד כְּיִחוּדוֹ

נֶעְלָם וְגַם אֵין סוֹף לְאַחְדוּתוֹ.

אֵין לוֹ דְּמוּת הַגּוּף וְאֵינוֹ גוּף

לֹא נַעֲרֹךְ אֵלָיו קְדֻשָּׁתוֹ.

קַדְמוֹן לְכָל דָּבָר אֲשֶׁר נִבְרָא

רִאשׁוֹן וְאֵין רֵאשִׁית לְרֵאשִׁיתוֹ.

הִנּוֹ אֲדוֹן עוֹלָם

וְכָל נוֹצָר יוֹרֶה גְדֻלָּתוֹ וּמַלְכוּתוֹ.

שֶׁפַע נְבוּאָתוֹ נְתָנוֹ

אֶל אַנְשֵׁי סְגֻלָּתוֹ וְתִפְאַרְתּוֹ.

לֹא קָם בְּיִשְׂרָאֵל כְּמֹשֶׁה עוֹד

נָבִיא וּמַבִּיט אֶת תְּמוּנָתוֹ.

תּוֹרַת אֱמֶת נָתַן לְעַמּוֹ אֵל

עַל יַד נְבִיאוֹ נֶאֱמַן בֵּיתוֹ.

לֹא יַחֲלִיף הָאֵל וְלֹא יָמִיר דָּתוֹ

לְעוֹלָמִים לְזוּלָתוֹ.

צוֹפֶה וְיוֹדֵעַ סְתָרֵינוּ

מַבִּיט לְסוֹף דָּבָר בְּקַדְמָתוֹ.

גּוֹמֵל לְאִישׁ חֶסֶד כְּמִפְעָלוֹ

נוֹתֵן לְרָשָׁע רָע כְּרִשְׁעָתוֹ.

יִשְׁלַח לְקֵץ יָמִין מְשִׁיחֵנוּ

לִפְדּוֹת מְחַכֵּי קֵץ יְשׁוּעָתוֹ.

מֵתִים יְחַיֶּה אֵל בְּרֹב חַסְדּוֹ

בָּרוּךְ עֲדֵי עַד שֵׁם תְּהִלָּתוֹ.

The Tefilla Text

Translation: *Great is the living God and praised. He exists, and His existence is beyond time. He is One, and there is no unity like His. Unfathomable, His Oneness is infinite. He has neither bodily form nor substance; His holiness is beyond compare. He preceded all that was created. He was first: there was no beginning to His beginning. Behold He is Master of the Universe; and every creature shows His greatness and majesty. The rich flow of His prophecy He gave to His treasured people in whom He gloried. Never in Israel has there arisen another like Moses, a prophet who beheld God's image. God gave His people a Torah of truth by the hand of His prophet, most faithful of His House. God will not alter or change His law for any other, for eternity. He sees and knows our secret thoughts; as soon as something is begun, He foresees its end. He rewards people with loving-kindness according to their deeds; He punishes the wicked according to his wickedness. At the end of days He will send our Messiah to redeem those who await His final salvation. God will revive the dead in His great loving-kindness. Blessed for evermore is His glorious name!*

Educational Themes contained in the text:

- Rambam's Thirteen Principles of Faith
  1. Belief in the existence of God.
  2. Belief in God's unity.
  3. Belief in God's incorporeality.
  4. Belief in God's eternity.
  5. The imperative to pray to God.
  6. Belief that God communicates with man through prophecy.
  7. Belief in the primacy of the prophecy of Moses.
  8. Belief in the divine origin of the Torah.
  9. Belief in the immutability of the Torah.
  10. Belief in God's omniscience.
  11. Belief in divine reward and punishment.
  12. Belief in the arrival of the Messiah.
  13. Belief in the resurrection of the dead.
- God = Creator, the God of history (*Hashgaḥa*)
- Revelation through Prophecy
- Moshe = archetypal prophet
- *Torah min hashamayim*

The Illustration

Due to the length of this *tefilla* it was logistically impossible to include in the page any educational elements other than the background texture which has an abstract and sublime feel to it to correspond to the words of this *tefilla* which describe a sublime God, and our familiar small bird. However, the contrast between the sublime and great God described in the words of this *tefilla*, and the tiniest and frailest of His creations in the illustration could be an interesting discussion to have with the children. Many of the characteristics described in the *tefilla*, based as it is on Rambam's Thirteen Principles of Faith, relate to the way that Hashem interacts with humans. Yet He also creates and sustains a myriad of other species, and this is an inspiring wonder for the children to reflect upon.

ברכות השחר 1
Morning Blessings 1

בָּרוּךְ אַתָּה יהוה
אֱלֹהֵינוּ מֶלֶךְ הָעוֹלָם
אֲשֶׁר נָתַן לַשֶּׂכְוִי בִינָה
לְהַבְחִין בֵּין יוֹם וּבֵין לָיְלָה.

בָּרוּךְ אַתָּה יהוה
אֱלֹהֵינוּ מֶלֶךְ הָעוֹלָם
שֶׁלֹּא עָשַׂנִי גּוֹי.

What special gifts has Hashem given you?

בָּרוּךְ אַתָּה יהוה
אֱלֹהֵינוּ מֶלֶךְ הָעוֹלָם
שֶׁלֹּא עָשַׂנִי עָבֶד.

"Hashem gave each of His creatures special gifts."

Boys say
בָּרוּךְ אַתָּה יהוה
אֱלֹהֵינוּ מֶלֶךְ הָעוֹלָם
שֶׁלֹּא עָשַׂנִי אִשָּׁה.

Girls say
בָּרוּךְ אַתָּה יהוה
אֱלֹהֵינוּ מֶלֶךְ הָעוֹלָם
שֶׁעָשַׂנִי כִּרְצוֹנוֹ.

The Tefilla Text

Translation: *Blessed are You, LORD our God, King of the Universe, who gives the heart understanding to distinguish day from night.*

Blessed are You, LORD our God, King of the Universe, who has not made me a heathen.

Blessed are You, LORD our God, King of the Universe, who has not made me a slave.

[Boys say:] *Blessed are You, LORD our God, King of the Universe, who has not made me a woman.*

[Girls say:] *Blessed are You, LORD our God, King of the Universe, who has made me according to His will.*

Educational Themes contained in the text:

• Who am I? (personal identity)

- Who would I like to be? What will I do with what I have been given?
- The ability to distinguish (between good and evil, light and dark, myself and others) is God given

- What are my unique talents and where did they come from?
- Is intelligence nature or nurture?
- What are my needs and who fulfills them?

The Illustration

The illustration presents us with the dawn of a new day, as we begin the Morning Blessings. Our attention is drawn to the central element of the illustration – the rooster (שכוי) who announces the dawning of a new day to the world. The word שכוי features in the first of the blessings, and is here translated as "heart" (taken from the Koren Sacks Siddur). This is the opinion of Rabbeinu Asher (the Rosh), who disagrees with Rashi's opinion that it means the rooster. The rooster has been given the ability to distinguish between night and day (and thus changes his behavior at dawn). This is a God-given ability programmed into his nature. If

we translate the word שכוי as heart, then we are reflecting on our own human abilities, which also come from Hashem. The illustration is asking the child to reflect on God as Creator of all species, each with its own abilities, and how this applies to us as well. The illustration can and should be considered in conjunction with both kavanot, which explore this further.

Note that the second icon of the navigation bar is now highlighted (the morning sun shining) signifying that we have entered the second section of the Shaḥarit service – the Morning Blessings.

The Kavanot

The Upper *Kavana*: *"Hashem gave each of His creatures special gifts."*

This is a direct quote from Rabbi S.R. Hirsch's commentary on the siddur, and asks the child to reflect on Hashem as Creator of the universe, including all the species contained therein, and how He created each one with wisdom. This means that each species has its own God-given nature and abilities that give them the best chance to survive and prosper, and with these they can benefit mankind (as with the case of the rooster, which serves as mankind's alarm clock!). The educator may wish to ask the children to brainstorm the abilities of different animals, and how these abilities help them survive and prosper, and benefit us. Then

the educator may wish to name "man" as the final creation to consider.

The Lower *Kavana*: *What special gifts has Hashem given you?*

This *kavana* asks the child to reflect on their own God-given abilities and builds on both the illustration and the upper *kavana*, encouraging personal reflection. . The child may consider other "gifts," apart from abilities and skills, such as material possessions, health, family, friends, privilege, etc. This should be encouraged, as the lesson of God providing for us can be learned from here as well.

בִּרְכוֹת הַשַּׁחַר 2
Morning Blessings 2

The Tefilla Text

Translation: *Blessed are You,* LORD *our God, King of the Universe, who gives sight to the blind.*

Blessed are You, LORD *our God, King of the Universe, who clothes the naked.*

Blessed are You, LORD *our God, King of the Universe, who sets captives free.*

Blessed are You, LORD *our God, King of the Universe, who raises those bowed down.*

Blessed are You, LORD *our God, King of the Universe, who spreads the earth above the waters.*

Blessed are You, LORD *our God, King of the Universe, who has provided me with all I need.*

The words פּוֹקֵחַ עִוְרִים in the first blessing are highlighted in brown, anchoring them to the lower *kavana*, as well as drawing the eye toward Dov. The words שֶׁעָשָׂה לִי כָּל צָרְכִּי are highlighted in green, and anchored to the upper *kavana*.

Educational Themes contained in the text:

- What are your needs?
- What do we need to thank Hashem for on a daily basis?

- Sub-themes:
- Gift of sight
- Dignity of clothing
- Appreciation of physical abilities/functioning
- Freedom

The Illustration

In this illustration, Dov is looking up at the first rays of sunlight of the morning, enjoying their feel on his face. As he appreciates the feeling of warmth, it is almost as if he is aware of the light for the first time. The illustration is inspired by the first of these blessings, which expresses gratitude to Hashem for sight, by blessing Him as פּוֹקֵחַ עִוְרִים. Perhaps as Dov's eyes are opened to the light, he is experiencing a moment of enlightenment to the themes contained in these blessings, generating a feeling of gratitude for all the gifts he has from Hashem. This is also an alternative way to understand the first blessing here: we thank Hashem not just for the ability to see, but also for enlightenment too, for opening our eyes to the truth.

The Kavanot

The Upper *Kavana: Do you have everything you need in life?*

This *kavana* asks the children to reflect on what they need to live a good life, where they get these things from, and whether they have them in their own life. Inspired by the blessings on this page and the next, where we list many of the things that we need and receive from God, we are asking the child to think about what these things are. This will lead to an exercise in values clarification (and the educator may wish to explore this in a creative way, using an educational activity such as an auction, balloon debate, or some other values clarification activity) where the child is encouraged to actually decide what is important in their life, and what is less important. The hope is that they will discard the less important things such as material possessions, and external goals, and focus on what is intrinsic to a happy life, such as health, family, love, meaning, etc. Once they have arrived at some kind of a list, the child can be asked to consider whether they have these in their life and where they come from. The final stage of this process is to be grateful for them. This helps the child to feel more connected to the Morning Blessings, as they realize that the aim of these blessings is to show gratitude for the important things in life.

The Lower *Kavana: Imagine seeing sunlight for the first time…*

This *kavana* asks the child to reflect on the gift of sight as well as to appreciate the beauty found in nature. This can be an experiential activity in the form of a creative imagination exercise (guided imagery). The educator can ask the children to close their eyes for a minute, and then to imagine they had never seen daylight. Now ask them to open their eyes, and describe the feeling of seeing daylight (or sunlight if this can be carried out outside on a sunny day) for the first time. This should lead to an appreciation for the gift of sight, as well as the beauty of nature.

ברכות השחר 3
Morning Blessings 3

בָּרוּךְ אַתָּה יהוה ¹
אֱלֹהֵינוּ מֶלֶךְ הָעוֹלָם ²
הַמֵּכִין מִצְעֲדֵי גָבֶר. ³

בָּרוּךְ אַתָּה יהוה ⁴
אֱלֹהֵינוּ מֶלֶךְ הָעוֹלָם ⁵
אוֹזֵר יִשְׂרָאֵל בִּגְבוּרָה. ⁶

בָּרוּךְ אַתָּה יהוה ⁷
אֱלֹהֵינוּ מֶלֶךְ הָעוֹלָם ⁸
עוֹטֵר יִשְׂרָאֵל בְּתִפְאָרָה. ⁹

בָּרוּךְ אַתָּה יהוה ¹⁰
אֱלֹהֵינוּ מֶלֶךְ הָעוֹלָם ¹¹
הַנּוֹתֵן לַיָּעֵף כֹּחַ. ¹²

Why does the Jewish people need strength?

"You should be strong like a lion when you get up in the morning to serve Hashem!"

The Tefilla Text

Translation: *Blessed are You,* LORD *our God, King of the Universe, who makes firm the steps of man.*

Blessed are You, LORD *our God, King of the Universe, who girds Israel with strength.*

Blessed are You, LORD *our God, King of the Universe, who crowns Israel with glory.*

Blessed are You, LORD *our God, King of the Universe, who gives strength to the weary.*

The words אוזר ישראל בגבורה are highlighted in green and anchored to the upper *kavana*.

Educational Themes contained in the text:

- What are your needs?
- What do we need to thank Hashem for on a daily basis?
- Sub-themes:

Strength (physical/spiritual)
Nature
National glory (achievements/talents of Israel)

The Illustration

The Lion, looking proudly out into the distance, is a beautiful expression of many of the themes found in the blessings on this page. He represents the strength given to the tired (כח הנותן ליעף), the strength (גבורה) given to Israel, and the lion's magnificent regal mane hints at the glory of the crown given to Israel (עוטר ישראל בתפארה). These concepts are abstract and difficult for a child of this age to fully understand. However, with the help of our illustrated lion, they can begin to understand what these concepts may mean in a more concrete way. An interesting side point to note (and perhaps bring to the children) is that the illustrator was inspired by the memorial in the cemetery in Tel Ḥai in northern Israel (see below) when drawing the lion. This memorial, known as "The Roaring Lion," memorializes Joseph Trumpeldor and seven other Jewish fighters who fell in the Battle for Tel Ḥai in 1920, commemorating their brave fight for the cause of Zionism in pre-State Palestine. Many consider them as the very first casualties of the Arab-Israel conflict, and Trumpeldor's bravery and heroism has become legendary in the history of modern Zionism. The educator may wish to briefly tell this story, and ask the children why they think a lion was chosen to memorialize the bravery and heroism of these fighters. This could be a thought-provoking way to then consider and explore the blessings on this page of the siddur.

The Kavanot

The Upper *Kavana*: *Why does the Jewish people need strength?*

This *kavana*, anchored to the words אוזר ישראל בגבורה, asks the child to reflect on what strength may mean, and why we would need to pray for it on a national level. Does this strength mean physical strength or spiritual strength? Do we need these on a personal level? If so, then why also ask for it on a national level? What challenges do we face nationally, that would necessitate a blessing thanking Hashem for providing national strength? This could be approached in the context of Jewish history (anti-Semitism and spiritual persecution) or contemporary times (the continued fight for the State of Israel or contemporary anti-Semitism, and the struggle against assimilation. If the educator chooses to focus on the former, the lion in the illustration and the story of Joseph Trumpeldor could be a direction to take). We thank Hashem for the strength to rise to these challenges, both physically and spiritually, and acknowledge that the necessary courage and bravery come from Him. It is interesting to note that in modern Hebrew the word גבורה is more commonly associated with meanings such as "courage" or "heroism", both forms of spiritual strength.

The Lower *Kavana*: *"You should be strong like a lion when you get up in the morning to serve Hashem!"*

This *kavana*, a paraphrased quote from the first line of the *Shulḥan Arukh*, asks the children to reflect on the necessary strength just to get up in the morning and face the day. A more positive spin can also be taken (more in line with the original intent of the *Shulḥan Arukh*), encouraging the children to fill their day with energy and enthusiasm to be a Jew and to carry out what Hashem asks of us – to be a good person and keep mitzvot. The educator may wish to ask the children why they think the *Shulḥan Arukh* chose a lion from which to learn this positive attitude? Does it take a strong heroic nature to approach life in such an upbeat positive way? Why? What characteristics does a lion have that we should try to emulate to be a good Jew? This may also be a good opportunity to explore the concept of living one's life according to the *Shulḥan Arukh*, and how halakha has advice for us in every area of our lives, from the day-to-day to the special occasions.

ברוך שאמר
Barukh SheAmar

33

1 בָּרוּךְ פּוֹדֶה וּמַצִּיל
2 בָּרוּךְ שְׁמוֹ
3 בָּרוּךְ אַתָּה יהוה אֱלֹהֵינוּ מֶלֶךְ הָעוֹלָם
4 הָאֵל הָאָב הָרַחֲמָן הַמְהֻלָּל בְּפִי עַמּוֹ
5 מְשֻׁבָּח וּמְפֹאָר בִּלְשׁוֹן חֲסִידָיו וַעֲבָדָיו
6 וּבְשִׁירֵי דָוִד עַבְדֶּךָ
7 נְהַלֶּלְךָ יהוה אֱלֹהֵינוּ.
8 בִּשְׁבָחוֹת וּבִזְמִירוֹת
9 נְגַדֶּלְךָ וּנְשַׁבֵּחֲךָ וּנְפָאֶרְךָ
10 וְנַזְכִּיר שִׁמְךָ וְנַמְלִיכְךָ
11 מַלְכֵּנוּ אֱלֹהֵינוּ, יָחִיד חֵי הָעוֹלָמִים
12 מֶלֶךְ, מְשֻׁבָּח וּמְפֹאָר עֲדֵי עַד שְׁמוֹ הַגָּדוֹל
13 בָּרוּךְ אַתָּה יהוה, מֶלֶךְ מְהֻלָּל בַּתִּשְׁבָּחוֹת.

32

Hold the front two צִיצִיּוֹת while saying this תְּפִלָּה and kiss them once you have finished.

1 בָּרוּךְ שֶׁאָמַר
2 וְהָיָה הָעוֹלָם, בָּרוּךְ הוּא.
3 בָּרוּךְ עוֹשֶׂה בְרֵאשִׁית
4 בָּרוּךְ אוֹמֵר וְעוֹשֶׂה
5 בָּרוּךְ גּוֹזֵר וּמְקַיֵּם
6 בָּרוּךְ מְרַחֵם עַל הָאָרֶץ
7 בָּרוּךְ מְרַחֵם עַל הַבְּרִיּוֹת
8 בָּרוּךְ מְשַׁלֵּם שָׂכָר טוֹב לִירֵאָיו
9 בָּרוּךְ חַי לָעַד וְקַיָּם לָנֶצַח

Choose a friend or family member and praise them for something. Now try it with Hashem.

The Tefilla Text

Translation: *Blessed is He who spoke and the world came into being, blessed is He. Blessed is He who creates the universe. Blessed is He who speaks and acts. Blessed is He who decrees and fulfills. Blessed is He who shows compassion to the earth. Blessed is He who shows compassion to all creatures. Blessed is He who gives a good reward to those who fear Him. Blessed is He who lives forever and exists to eternity. Blessed is He who redeems and saves. Blessed is His name. Blessed are You, LORD our God, King of the Universe, God, compassionate Father, extolled by the mouth of His people, praised and glorified by the tongue of His devoted ones and those who serve Him. With the songs of Your servant David we will praise You, O LORD our God. With praises and psalms we will magnify and praise You, glorify You, Speak Your name and proclaim Your kingship, our King, our God, the only One, Giver of life to the worlds, the King whose great name is praised and glorified to all eternity. Blessed are You, LORD, the King extolled with songs of praise.*

The words בשבחות ובזמירות נגדלך ונשבחך ונפארך are highlighted in light brown to anchor them to the *kavana*.

Educational Themes contained in the text:

- Praising God – what would you praise God for?
- *Zimra* = song/poetry

- God as Creator of the universe
- God as the God of history (השגחה כללית ופרטית)
- Reward and punishment
- The songs of David HaMelekh

The Illustration

Due to the length of this *tefilla* constraints were placed on the illustration. The illustrator therefore chose an understated and simple illustration of our small recurring bird, as well as a branch of a tree in blossom, both beautiful in their simplicity. These contrast with the lofty nature of the *tefilla*, which speaks of sublime and grand concepts, such as God as Creator of the world, His Divine Providence in the world, governing with compassion and reward. These lofty ideas are high-lighted by the smallest of creations found in the illustration: the simple bird and flower. Yet the mighty God was concerned with their creation and sustenance as much as He is with entire nations and worlds.

Note the third icon in the navigation bar, the musical note, is now highlighted, signifying that we have entered the third section of *Tefillat Shaḥarit – Pesukei DeZimra*.

The Kavana

Choose a friend or family member and praise them for something.

Now try it with Hashem.

This *kavana* asks the child to reflect on what it means to praise, and how we give praise. It asks the child to experience the process involved in praise, in choosing the words, in feeling the emotions of humbling one-self to praise another, and watching how being praised affects the other person as well. The most important aspect of this *kavana* is that it presents the child with a concrete way to understand the abstract concept of praising the sublime God. Starting with a friend or family, and then moving on to God, this empowers the child to write their own *tefillot* to Hashem, and encourages them to speak to Hashem in a direct and personal way in a language in which they are fluent. This could be a transformative experience.

אשרי
Ashrei

The Tefilla Text

Translation: *Happy are those who dwell in Your House; they shall continue to praise You, Selah!*

Happy are the people for whom this is so; happy are the people whose God is the LORD.

You open Your hand, and satisfy every living thing with favor.

The words אשרי are highlighted in red, and anchored to the word "happy" in the upper *kavana*. The verse

פותח את ידך ומשביע לכל חי רצון is highlighted in green and anchored to the lower *kavana*.

Educational Themes contained in the text:

- First verse = quiet meditation
- "Your House" = Temple/*Beit Kenesset*
- God is source of all blessing in the world and in our lives
- Happiness = serving/closeness to/relationship with God
- First verse = individual; second verse = nation

The Illustration

This illustration focuses the child on the critical verse in this *tefilla* and the whole of *Pesukei DeZimra* – פותח את ידך ומשביע לכל חי רצון. Ellie and Dov are sitting in an ancient olive tree (olive trees, native to *Eretz Yisrael* and one of the seven species, typically live to an old age, with some living as long as 2000 years!) and staring out to an ancient synagogue. The olive tree represents Hashem sustaining us through nature, and Ellie and Dov show they are truly connected to nature, sitting comfortably in the tree. Our friend the bird, perched on a top branch of the tree, is a testament to Hashem's role as sustainer not just to humans but to all of His creatures. However, the tree and its hidden roots, together with the ancient synagogue, demonstrate that as well as physical sustenance, spiritual sustenance is also vital, and that is also provided to us by Hashem through His Torah and the Land of Israel.

Moreover, the first verse in this *tefilla* is also expressed in the illustration. According to Rabbi S.R. Hirsch, the use of the word יושבי rather than יושבים suggests that the people that are truly happy and fulfilled are those that are frequently sitting in "Your House" (which could be the *Beit HaMikdash* in Jerusalem, or the *Beit Kenesset*, such as the one in the illustration), but not at the present moment (which would have required the word יושבים). These people, who draw their inspiration from "Your House," are found outside of it most of the time, like Ellie and Dov in the illustration here, because they are firmly living in the outside world. Their values, while drawn from the Torah and the world of the yeshiva and synagogue, need to be lived in the outside world to be fulfilled and actualized. True spiritual growth is taking the experiences from the house of worship into the outside world, into everyday life.

The Kavanot

The Upper *Kavana*: *What makes you happy?*

This *kavana* asks the child to reflect on happiness in their life. It does not necessarily encourage them to think about the *tefilla Ashrei*, or God, or even Judaism. Every child understands happiness and what makes them happy. Once this discussion has run its course, the educator should then link it to the words of the *tefilla* – why would having a connection to Hashem cause happiness?

The Lower *Kavana*: *Where do all the things in your life that you need come from?*

This *kavana*, anchored to the verse פותח את ידך ומשביע לכל חי רצון, asks the child to reflect on the source of all the important things in their life. Of course the ultimate answer is God, and this is the goal of the educator. However, this may not be reachable immediately in the mind of the children, and many other answers should be deemed as acceptable, such as parents, other family members, teachers, friends, other authorities, etc. The ultimate goal of the educator should be to encourage the child to understand that despite the important role of these agencies, our sustenance ultimately comes from God.

ישתבח
Yishtabaḥ

The Tefilla Text

Translation: *May Your name be praised forever, our King, the great and holy God, King in heaven and on earth. For to You,* LORD *our God and God of our ancestors, it is right to offer song and praise, hymn and psalm, strength and dominion, eternity, greatness and power, song of praise and glory, holiness and kingship, blessings and thanks, from now and forever. Blessed are You,* LORD, *God and King, exalted in praises, God of thanksgivings, Master of wonders, who delights in hymns of song, King, God, Giver of life to the worlds.*

The word ישתבח is highlighted in blue and anchored to the lower kavana, and the words בשירי זמרה are highlighted in light brown and anchored to the upper *kavana* that speaks about song.

Educational Themes contained in the text:

- The impossible task of praising Hashem
- Hashem's name
- *Malkhut*/God as King
- אדון הנפלאות
- *Zimra* = song/poetry
- The role of song and music in prayer

The Illustration

This illustration focuses on the impact of song and music in our *tefilla*. With the words בשירי זמרה and שיר ושבחה in this *tefilla*, the role of song and music is clearly important to the process of praising God. Music refreshes and nourishes the soul, uplifting us and bringing us closer to Hashem. This is beautifully expressed in the illustration with Ellie flying her kite (its musical notes representing song) outside in nature. The music together with nature has Ellie's kite, or soul, soaring and being drawn to heaven, as she aspires to become closer to Hashem. The pull of song as a transformative experience is so strong it looks like it may pull Ellie off her feet as the kite draws closer and closer to the sky. Note also the windswept plants, representing nature testifying to the power of the spirit. Perhaps the wind itself is making its own music as a way to praise God, and this can be seen in the musical notes found in the sky.

The Kavanot

The Upper *Kavana*: *How do you feel when you sing?*

This *kavana* asks the child to reflect on the relationship between song and *tefilla*. This *tefilla* makes a clear link between the concept of praise and song/music. Music and song can impact deeply on our emotions; they can also be a way to express our emotions. It is a hard task to find sufficient words to express gratitude to Hashem for all that He gives us. That is why we rely on the words of the *tefillot* in our siddur. But sometimes, the words may not be enough to capture the emotional outpouring of gratitude that we have, and so we turn to song. And sometimes, to encourage us to find the appropriate emotions with which to approach the impossible task of praising Hashem, we turn to music. These are all difficult concepts for a young child to comprehend, but they can understand what happens to their mood when they sing or listen to music. And so, from this question, a child can reflect on the role of music on their life, and how it can help us say nice things about Hashem.

The Lower *Kavana*: *Does Hashem need us to tell Him how great He is? Why is it important to praise Hashem?*

This *kavana* asks the child to connect to Hashem as a great and powerful independent force that does not have human emotions. It also asks the child to reflect on the role and impact of *tefilla* in their own lives. These questions should be considered separately and in turn. The first stage is to ask the children to consider what God is and what He isn't. He doesn't need our praise because He is all-powerful and all-knowing. He is not dependent on other people's compliments (as we are). In which case, why do we bother? Here we now ask the children to consider that *tefilla* may be as much about ourselves as it is about Hashem. Standing in front of someone and praising and thanking them is a transformative and humbling experience. We need that experience more for us than for Hashem. This is in fact expressed in the very verb used to pray in Hebrew – להתפלל – which is in a reflexive construct – it is something that happens to us. When we verbalize all the things we need to thank and praise God for, we go through a transformative experience whereby we internalize just how dependent we are on Him, and this should also regulate our opinions and behavior in this light.

אור חדש
Or Ḥadash

39

בָּרוּךְ אַתָּה יהוה [1]

אֱלֹהֵינוּ מֶלֶךְ הָעוֹלָם [2]

יוֹצֵר אוֹר וּבוֹרֵא חֹשֶׁךְ [3]

עֹשֶׂה שָׁלוֹם וּבוֹרֵא אֶת הַכֹּל. [4]

הַמֵּאִיר לָאָרֶץ וְלַדָּרִים עָלֶיהָ [5]

בְּרַחֲמִים [6]

וּבְטוּבוֹ מְחַדֵּשׁ בְּכָל יוֹם תָּמִיד [7]

מַעֲשֵׂה בְרֵאשִׁית. [8]

אוֹר חָדָשׁ עַל צִיּוֹן תָּאִיר [9]

וְנִזְכֶּה כֻלָּנוּ מְהֵרָה לְאוֹרוֹ. [10]

בָּרוּךְ אַתָּה יהוה [11]

יוֹצֵר הַמְּאוֹרוֹת. [12]

38

Which direction are you facing now while you are praying? Why?

"The glory of Hashem can be felt in the rays of sunshine from the morning sun."

The Tefilla Text

Translation: *Blessed are You, LORD our God, King of the Universe, who forms light and creates darkness, makes peace and creates all. In compassion He gives light to the earth and its inhabitants, and in His goodness continually renews the work of creation, day after day.*

May You make a new light shine over Zion, and may we all soon be worthy of its light. Blessed are You, LORD, who forms the radiant lights.

The words אור חדש על ציון תאיר ונזכה כלנו מהרה לאורו are highlighted in brown to visually anchor them to the upper *kavana*, as well as the illustration of Jerusalem.

Educational Themes contained in the text:

- Light vs. dark (day and night) – both come from God
- God found in the rays of the morning sun
- Light = new life; wisdom; happiness; (Dark =

suffering; failure; death; and these also come from God –see Berakhot 11b)
- Light = harmony vs. Darkness = confusion (see Isaiah 45:7)

- *Or Ḥadash* = original light of creation
- *Tziyon* – Jerusalem
- A New Light on Jerusalem (Messianic times, the New City of Jerusalem)

The Illustration

This illustration explores the concept of light in various forms and meanings, as well as Jerusalem (the word ציון as found in the text of the *tefilla* is another name for Jerusalem), and the connection between the two. The center of the illustration is Jerusalem on a hilltop, with an imposing *Beit HaMikdash* towering over the city in stature and influence. Both *Eretz Yisrael* and Jerusalem are considered to be higher in physical geography and spiritual stature (See Rashi on Shemot 33:1 and Devarim. 1:25). The educator may wish to use the illustration to talk about the term עליה, which is used in the Talmud to refer both to moving to *Eretz Yisrael*, as well as to Jerusalem (from elsewhere in *Eretz Yisrael*). Ellie sits on a rock admiring the beauty and spiritual influence of the city from the foreground of the scene.

From behind the city a bright light emanates. It is not clear if this light is coming from the sun, obscured by the buildings, or another source entirely, such as the city itself, or directly from Hashem. This light could be Hashem's Divine Presence that exists in the holy city of Jerusalem, or it could represent Hashem's protection, or the light of enlightenment from the Torah (כי

מציון תצא תורה ודבר ה׳ מירושלים). This light links the two parts of the text found on the page – Hashem is the Creator of light, and His holy city of Jerusalem spreads light across the world. The light referred to in the *tefilla* could be light from the sun, or a spiritual light, just as the light in the illustration could come from the obscured sun, or from another spiritual source. That spiritual light, from which the world benefits, could be directly from God, from the people of Israel as an אור לגוים, or from the Torah (כי נר מצוה ותורה אור). Or it could be a combination of all of these – the Jewish people, living in Jerusalem and *Eretz Yisrael*, as a model nation, serving as a light unto the other nations, through keeping the Torah. A "new light" over Jerusalem could also refer to Messianic times, when Jerusalem will be rebuilt. Perhaps Messianic times will only be ushered in once all of these concepts are brought together.

Note that the fourth icon of the navigation bar is now highlighted (a person saying the *Shema* at their desk) signifying that we have entered the fourth section of the *Shaḥarit* service – the *Shema* and its blessings.

The Kavanot

The Upper *Kavana*: *Which direction are you facing now while you are praying? Why?*

This *kavana* asks the child to reflect on the relationship between Jerusalem/Israel and *tefilla*, and to form a connection to the Land of Israel through *tefilla*. Although there is every chance the children's *tefilla* is not in a synagogue, but rather in a classroom or other space that does not necessarily face towards *mizraḥ* (literally eastward – toward the Land of Israel), this is a good opportunity to introduce the children to the concept of praying in the direction of the land of Israel. According to halakha (*Berakhot* 30a; *Shulḥan Arukh*

94:1) while the direction faced during other prayers is less important, one must face the Land of Israel when praying the *Amida*. If one is praying inside the Land of Israel, then one must pray facing Jerusalem. It has therefore become the custom to place the *Aron Kodesh* on the wall of the synagogue that faces Jerusalem, so that when one prays the *Amida*, one is facing Jerusalem and the *Aron* at the same time. But when this cannot be achieved for logistical reasons, praying toward Jerusalem takes precedence (*Mishna Berura* 94:10).

This is the first *tefilla* in the siddur (but not the last – see also the *Amida* on page 50 and the removal of the

Torah from the *Aron* on page 66) in which we focus our attentions to Jerusalem. This *kavana* asks the children to reflect on why. The educator may wish to explore the concept that while we believe God is incorporeal and cannot be contained by any single location, He allows His Presence to be concentrated in one location – Jerusalem and the Temple there – so we can conceptualize Him (for otherwise it is too hard for a human being to focus on God during *tefilla*).

The Lower *Kavana*: *"The glory of Hashem can be felt in the rays of sunshine from the morning sun."*

This *kavana* asks the child to connect to Hashem through the world around them, especially through light, and the rays of sunshine. It is a quote from Rabbi S.R. Hirsch's commentary on the siddur. This quote brings many of the ideas intimated in the illustration together, such as the light emanating from Hashem's presence as well as from the sun. The educator could use this as a great opportunity to take the children outside to experience the rays of sun or nature in general, and meditate on finding and connecting to God's presence within it. Alternatively, this could be a good opportunity for a guided imagination exercise, where the children are asked to imagine and experience the rays of sun on their face (the children should have their eyes closed and be guided by the educator to a place in their imagination where they can feel the rays of the sun on their face. They can then discuss what it felt like etc.).

אהבה רבה
Ahava Raba

אַהֲבָה רַבָּה אֲהַבְתָּנוּ

יהוה אֱלֹהֵינוּ

חֶמְלָה גְדוֹלָה וִיתֵרָה חָמַלְתָּ עָלֵינוּ.

אָבִינוּ, הָאָב הָרַחֲמָן, הַמְרַחֵם

רַחֵם עָלֵינוּ

וְתֵן בְּלִבֵּנוּ לְהָבִין וּלְהַשְׂכִּיל

לִשְׁמֹעַ, לִלְמֹד וּלְלַמֵּד,

לִשְׁמֹר וְלַעֲשׂוֹת, וּלְקַיֵּם

אֶת כָּל דִּבְרֵי תַלְמוּד תּוֹרָתֶךָ בְּאַהֲבָה.

בָּרוּךְ אַתָּה יהוה

הַבּוֹחֵר בְּעַמּוֹ יִשְׂרָאֵל

בְּאַהֲבָה.

Whom do you love?

"It is a mitzva to love and respect the wonderful and awesome Hashem."

The Tefilla Text

Translation: *You have loved us with great love,* LORD *our God, and with surpassing compassion have You had compassion on us.*

Our Father, compassionate Father, ever compassionate, have compassion on us. Instill in our hearts the desire to understand and discern, to listen, learn and teach, to observe, perform and fulfill all the teachings of Your Torah in love.

Blessed are You, LORD, *who chooses His people Israel in love.*

The words אהבה רבה אהבתנו have been highlighted in brown and visually anchored to the upper *kavana*, and to the word "love" in the lower *kavana*, and the *sefer Torah* and walls of Jerusalem in the illustration.

Educational Themes contained in the text:

- God's love for us
- Because of His love He gave us His Torah and chose us as a nation
- Chosenness, love, and being an *"Am Segula"*

The Illustration

This illustration focuses on the gifts that Hashem gives us, as an expression of His love for us. In this case, they are nature, the Torah, and Jerusalem/*Eretz Yisrael*. Each one is seen in the illustration, with our small bird representing nature. God and His love is a very abstract concept for any of us to understand. Rambam says that we can't hope to understand the essence of an infinite God, but we can understand Him through His creations and actions (*Mishneh Torah*, Laws of the Foundations of Torah 2:1–2; see the lower *kavana*). God's creations and gifts to us are an expression of His love for us. And understanding God's love, as expressed through His gifts, will in turn bring us to love Him. The illustration explores these themes and was inspired by the essay "Discourse on Loving Kindness," written by Rabbi E.E. Dessler, which explores the relationship between love and giving:

Here we come to an interesting question. We see that love and giving always come together. Is the giving a conse-quence of the love or is perhaps the reverse true: is the love a result of the giving? [...] Giving may bring about love for the same reason that a person loves what he himself has created or nurtured: he recognizes in it part of himself...

That which a person gives to another is never lost. It is an extension of his own being. He can see a part of himself in the fellow man to whom he has given. This is the attachment between one man and his fellow to which we give the name 'love.'"

In the illustration, we have joyful expressions of love on the faces of the children as they dance with the Torah, celebrate Jerusalem and the Land of Israel, and admire nature (the return of our friend the bird). The themes of Torah and the Land of Israel are also found in the text of this *tefilla* (although returning to the land is the part of the text that is omitted in this siddur). Through Hashem's gifts to us we can connect to Him with love and appreciation.

The Kavanot

The Upper *Kavana*: *Whom do you love?*

This *kavana* asks the child to reflect on what love is, and what it feels like to love God, by asking the child to reflect on the love that comes most naturally to them in their lives. While there is no wrong answer here, and all possibilities are educational opportunities, the most expected responses are parents and wider family, friends, pets, and even teachers. The educator should use the answers to explore why these people were chosen as those that the children love, how they express that love, and then relate these aspects of their love to the love of God.

The Lower *Kavana*: "*It is a mitzva to love and respect the wonderful and awesome Hashem.*"

This *kavana* is a quote from Rambam's *Mishneh Torah* (Laws of the Foundations of Torah 2:1–2). The *kavana* leads the child to reflect on what it means to love God. This will hopefully encourage connection to God. It complements the other *kavana* as well as the illustration. Each one aims to encourage the child to think about love in a concrete way until they are ready to be faced with the more abstract questions "What does it mean to love God? How do we love God? Why should we love God?" This quote can point toward those questions.

שמע 1
Shema 1

The Tefilla Text

Translation: *Listen, Israel: the LORD is our God, the LORD is One.*

Love the LORD your God with all your heart, with all your soul, and with all your might. These words which I command you today shall be on your heart. Teach them repeatedly to your children, speaking of them when you sit at home and when you travel on the way, when you lie down and when you rise. Bind them as a sign on your hand, and they shall be an emblem between your eyes. Write them on the doorposts of your house and gates.

The first line of the *Shema* is highlighted in brown and anchored to the upper *kavana*. The final letter of the first word – ע – and the final letter for the last word – ד – are highlighted in dark brown and anchored to the lower *kavana*.

The text of the *Shema* (all three paragraphs) has the cantillation marks (*ta'amei hamikra*) included in the text as this is often sung with this special tune even during *tefilla*. This is a good opportunity for the educator to explain what these are and even teach the notes to the children.

Educational Themes contained in the text:

- עול מלכות שמים – committing to having Hashem in our lives
- Hashem (Who is Hashem?)
- *Malkhut* – God's Kingship
- Love – love of God
- Jewish education – teaching Torah to young children
- *Tefillin*

The Illustration

This illustration is purely instructional. Dov is in school at his desk saying the first paragraph of the *Shema*. He is covering his eyes just as the rubric on the page directs him, and holding his *tzitzit* in preparation for the third paragraph of the *Shema*. The illustration can be used by the educator to explore with the children the reasons why we might cover our eyes for the first line of the *Shema*, and therefore the nature of the statement שמע ישראל.

The Kavanot

The Upper *Kavana*: *If you were asked to make a very important announcement, what would it be?*

This *kavana* focuses on the importance of announcements and declarations. It asks the child to find an announcement they would like everyone to be aware of (for example which sports team is their favorite, what they think of their teacher, their love for their pet). From here the educator can explore with the children what it feels like to declare something they really believe is important. For whom are they making the announcement and whom are they affecting when they make an announcement like that? Other people or themselves? The answer is of course both, and that is the impact the first line of the *Shema* has, and the reason we say it aloud.

The Lower *Kavana*: *Look at the two letters that are bigger than the rest. What do they spell? How are we being that when we say the שמע?*

The two letters that are larger than the others and are here highlighted, spell the word עד – witness. This implies that we are testifying as witnesses that God is One. Obviously the unity of God is too difficult a philosophical concept for this age group to grapple with. But the children can understand that when we say the *Shema* we are making a statement that we believe with absolute certainty that there is only one Hashem, and He is our Hashem. The educator at this point may wish to explore how we define God and what it means to be infinite.

שמע 2
Shema 2

> "Avraham was chosen not because he was righteous but because he was a teacher."

The Tefilla Text

Translation: *If you indeed heed My commandments with which I charge you today, to love the LORD your God and worship Him with all your heart and with all your soul, I will give rain in your land in its season, the early and late rain; and you shall gather in your grain, wine and oil. I will give grass in your field for your cattle, and you shall eat and be satisfied. Be careful lest your heart be tempted and you go astray and worship other gods, bowing down to them. Then the LORD's anger will flare against you and He will close the heavens so that there will be no rain. The land will not yield its crops, and you will perish swiftly from the good land that the LORD is giving you. Therefore, set these, My words, on your heart and soul. Bind them as a sign on your hand, and they shall be an emblem between your eyes. Teach them to your children, speaking of them when you sit at home and when you travel on the way, when you lie down and when you rise. Write them on the doorposts of your house and gates, so that you and your children may live long in the land that the LORD swore to your ancestors to give them, for as long as the heavens are above the earth.*

The words וְלִמַּדְתֶּם אֹתָם אֶת בְּנֵיכֶם are highlighted in red, and anchored to the lower *kavana*, and to the mother's dress.

Educational Themes contained in the text:

- עוֹל מִצְוֹת – committing to Hashem to do His mitzvot

- Love – love of God
- Hashem as source of all blessings and prosperity
- *Mezuza*
- *Tefillin*
- Reward for mitzvot
- Israel as a reward for doing mitzvot

The Illustration

While there are many different themes in this second paragraph of the *Shema* that could be explored with children, both the illustration and the single *kavana* found on this page consider the mitzva of teaching Torah to the next generation – וְלִמַּדְתֶּם אֹתָם אֶת בְּנֵיכֶם. Therefore these words are highlighted in red to link them to both the *kavana* and the illustration (the red of the mother's dress). This mitzva, to teach the words of Torah to one's children, is beautifully expressed in the illustration with Dov and Ellie's mother learning Torah with them on the couch in their home (if you look carefully at the text they are learning you can see it is the *Shema*, printed in the famous Koren font!).

The Kavana

"Avraham was chosen not because he was righteous but because he was a teacher."

This *kavana* asks the child to reflect on just how central the mitzva of teaching and education is to Judaism and the Torah. This is a quote from Rabbi J. Sacks in his book *A Letter in the Scroll*. This quote leads us to differentiate between learning Torah and teaching Torah. As well as making it clear that Avraham's election as progenitor of the Jewish people was not solely down to his righteous character, Rabbis Sacks is also suggesting that Avraham was not chosen because he was learned or a scholar, but rather because he was an educator – someone that understood the importance of education and how critical it is to teach the next generation. In fact, implied in the Torah is that not only Avraham's election as progenitor of Judaism and the Jewish people, but the election of the Jewish people to be a blessing to the world is down to the fact that this people will understand the importance of education.

Rabbi Sacks understands this from the verse in *Bereshit* (18:18–19):

וְאַבְרָהָם הָיוֹ יִהְיֶה לְגוֹי גָּדוֹל, וְעָצוּם; וְנִבְרְכוּ-בוֹ כֹּל, גּוֹיֵי הָאָרֶץ.

Abraham shall surely become a great and mighty nation, and all the nations of the earth shall be blessed in him.

כִּי יְדַעְתִּיו, לְמַעַן אֲשֶׁר יְצַוֶּה אֶת-בָּנָיו וְאֶת-בֵּיתוֹ אַחֲרָיו, וְשָׁמְרוּ דֶּרֶךְ יְהוָה, לַעֲשׂוֹת צְדָקָה וּמִשְׁפָּט--לְמַעַן, הָבִיא יְהוָה עַל-אַבְרָהָם, אֵת אֲשֶׁר-דִּבֶּר, עָלָיו.

For I have known him, to the end that he may command his children and his household after him, that they may keep the way of the LORD, to do righteousness and justice; to the end that the LORD may bring upon Abraham that which He hath spoken of him. (The educator might also want to draw attention to the *kavana* on page 18 on the בִּרְכוֹת הַתּוֹרָה which explores the relationship between the election of the Jewish people and their bringing blessing to the world, as promised to Avraham.)

The educator could explore this *kavana* with questions such as what was Avraham chosen for? What does righteous mean? How do we know Avraham was in fact righteous? Why do you think being a teacher (even just teaching your own children as a parent) is so important? Do you think you might one day become a teacher? Why? Why not?

שמע 3
Shema 3

Why is remembering important? What do you remember that is important to you?

"Remember the day when you came out of the land of Egypt all the days of your life" (*Devarim* 16:3).

The Tefilla Text

Translation: *The LORD spoke to Moses, saying: Speak to the Israelites and tell them to make tassels on the corners of their garments for all generations. They shall attach to the tassel at each corner a thread of blue. This shall be your tassel, and you shall see it and remember all of the LORD's commandments and keep them, not straying after your heart and after your eyes, following your own sinful desires. Thus you will be reminded to keep all My commandments, and be holy to your God. I am the LORD your God, who brought you out of the land of Egypt to be your God. I am the LORD your God.*

True

The two words with the root זכר (תזכרו and וזכרתם) are highlighted in green and anchored to the words "remembering" and "remember" in the upper *kavana*, which are also highlighted in green. The words הוצאתי אתכם מארץ מצרים are highlighted in brown, and anchored to the lower *kavana*.

Educational Themes contained in the text:

- *Yetziat Mitzrayim*
- *Tzitzit* as a reminder of the mitzvot

The Illustration

This illustration asks the child to reflect on the story of the exodus from Egypt, and helps the child to imagine this by presenting an exodus scene. In the background of the illustration the pyramids represent Egypt and slavery, and in the foreground we find Israelites leaving Egypt, carrying their belongings with them. We find Ellie (or an ancestor that looks like Ellie), intimating that we were all there and had that experience, whether as the Midrash suggests, our *neshamot* were actually there (at Mount Sinai immediately afterwards) or

that the experience of slavery and redemption is built into our national conscience. This also can be related to the famous concept expressed in the Haggada that if the Israelites hadn't been brought out by Hashem then we would still be slaves to Pharaoh today – וְאִלּוּ לֹא הוֹצִיא הַקָּדוֹשׁ בָּרוּךְ הוּא אֶת אֲבוֹתֵינוּ מִמִּצְרַיִם, הֲרֵי אָנוּ וּבָנֵינוּ וּבְנֵי בָנֵינוּ מְשֻׁעְבָּדִים הָיִינוּ לְפַרְעֹה בְּמִצְרָיִם. The translation of this is the *kavana* on the following page spread, and the same discussion can be had there (as Dov is featured in a depiction of the splitting of the Reed Sea).

The Kavanot

The Upper *Kavana*: *Why is remembering important? What do you remember that is important to you?*

This *kavana* asks the child to reflect on the everyday occurrence of remembering in their lives. Why is it important? What would life be like without the ability to remember? The educator may wish to begin with the question, "What things do you need to remember every day?" and start the conversation with the micro – the child's everyday life. From here, it is easy to move on to the larger concepts that even a child can understand why it is important to remember, such as their own identity (family, religion, where you live, etc.). Then the educator should bring the discussion around to the instruction to remember the mitzvot mentioned in the third paragraph of the *Shema*. Why and how do we remember all the mitzvot? What other things does the Torah ask us to remember (that Hashem created the world and took us out of Egypt – see the lower *kavana* and *Kiddush* on Friday night on page 82 of the siddur)? And finally, why do you think Hashem asks us to remember specifically these things?

The Lower *Kavana*: *"Remember the day when you came out of the land of Egypt all the days of your life"* (*Devarim 16:3*).

This *kavana* asks the child to reflect on the link between remembering the mitzvot and the exodus, and the fact that while we are only asked to remember mitzvot in the third paragraph of the *Shema* (by wearing *tzitzit*), the exodus is also mentioned there. What is the connection between these two and why are we asked to remember them both? The exodus from Egypt led to the giving of the Torah (mitzvot) on Mount Sinai. We could not have had one without the other, and we are asked to understand and always remember that. But perhaps the essence of Judaism was learnt in the exodus experience (no people should be slaves to another/Hashem is Creator and Master of the world and the God of history) and actualized into a way of living through the mitzvot. Together these two concepts/events are the essence of Judaism and how God expects us to live our lives.

גאל ישראל
Ga'al Yisrael

וְיַצִּיב, וְנָכוֹן וְקַיָּם ₁

וְיָשָׁר וְנֶאֱמָן ₂

וְאָהוּב וְחָבִיב, וְנֶחְמָד וְנָעִים ₃

וְנוֹרָא וְאַדִּיר ₄

וּמְתֻקָּן וּמְקֻבָּל, וְטוֹב וְיָפֶה ₅

הַדָּבָר הַזֶּה עָלֵינוּ לְעוֹלָם וָעֶד. ₆

בָּרוּךְ אַתָּה יהוה ₇

גָּאַל יִשְׂרָאֵל. ₈

What words would you use to describe Hashem?

"And if Hashem had not brought our fathers out of Egypt, then we would still be slaves to Pharaoh in Egypt today."

The Tefilla Text

Translation: *And firm, established and enduring, right, faithful, beloved, cherished, delightful, pleasant, awesome, mighty, perfect, accepted, good and beautiful is this faith for us for ever.*

Blessed are You, LORD, *who redeemed Israel.*

The words גאל ישראל are highlighted in aqua and anchored to the illustration (the Reed Sea) as well as the lower *kavana*.

Educational Themes contained in the text:

- Truth
- Faith
- Describing God
- Redemption
- Exodus
- Link between previous redemptions (*Shema* = exodus) and future redemption (*Amida* = Messianic redemption)

The Illustration

This illustration asks the child to reflect on the link between the historical redemption of the exodus from Egypt and the future Messianic redemption. The text on this page is taken from the section in the siddur between the *Shema* and the *Amida*. This is the transition between the description of the historical redemption of the exodus from Egypt (found in the third paragraph of the *Shema*), and the prayer for our future redemption, which is the theme of several of the blessings in the *Amida*. The illustration, a depiction of the splitting of the Reed Sea, as the Israelites finally leave Egypt and complete the exodus story, reflects the same bridge between these two redemptions. The previous page spread in the siddur was a general depiction of the Jews leaving Egypt, with Ellie's character present there. Here on this page, we have Dov leading the Israelites through the divided Reed Sea. Note that he is holding his biblical style hat exposing his modern "*kipa seruga*" (crocheted *kipa*), synonymous with a modern Religious Zionist outlook. While these Israelites are firmly on their way to the Land of Israel for the first time as a nation, Dov's *kipa* is a subtle hint toward the future redemptions, when the Jewish people will be gathered from all over the world and brought back to the Land of Israel, heralding the Messianic age. The placement of Dov in the illustration, or an ancestor that appears to look like Dov, can inspire the same ideas discussed in the previous illustration, that on some level all of our *neshamot* were present at this critical point in history (see above for a more detailed exploration of this). For this reason, the quote from the Haggada was chosen for the lower *kavana*.

The Kavanot

The Upper *Kavana*: *What words would you use to describe Hashem?*

This *kavana* asks the child to connect to Hashem through words. While the greatest Jewish philosophers throughout Jewish history have struggled to find adequate words to explore the essence of a sublime transcendent God, we should not underestimate how important the process is, and how competent a child even of this age could be in finding their own words. The process itself is important and transformative. The educator may wish to do this in a group using volunteers, or with each child in turn, or in pairs, or by asking the children to write down their words.

The Lower *Kavana*: *"And if Hashem had not brought our fathers out of Egypt, then we would still be slaves to Pharaoh in Egypt today."*

This *kavana* asks the child to connect to the historical exodus story in a personal way; to reflect on how their life has been affected in a personal (as well as national) way by this narrative. As we discussed in the previous illustration where we saw Ellie (or an ancestor that looks like Ellie) coming out of Egypt with the Children of Israel, here we have Dov leading them through the splitting of the Reed Sea. This gives us a springboard to explore this idea – that we (or our *neshamot*) were all there and had that experience. This *kavana* is a paraphrased translation of the quote from the Haggada – וְאִלּוּ לֹא הוֹצִיא הַקָּדוֹשׁ בָּרוּךְ הוּא אֶת אֲבוֹתֵינוּ מִמִּצְרַיִם, הֲרֵי אָנוּ וּבָנֵינוּ וּבְנֵי בָנֵינוּ מְשֻׁעְבָּדִים הָיִינוּ לְפַרְעֹה בְּמִצְרַיִם. The educator may wish to explore with the children exactly how the story has affected their lives (such as their identity, their values, rituals in their religion, etc.) as well as the more literal approach to this quote.

אבות
Avot

The עֲמִידָה (pages 50–63) is said standing with feet together. Before you begin, take three steps forward to mentally prepare to stand before Hashem.

1. אֲדֹנָי, שְׂפָתַי תִּפְתָּח, וּפִי יַגִּיד תְּהִלָּתֶךָ:

2. בָּרוּךְ אַתָּה יהוה

3. אֱלֹהֵינוּ וֵאלֹהֵי אֲבוֹתֵינוּ

4. אֱלֹהֵי אַבְרָהָם, אֱלֹהֵי יִצְחָק

5. וֵאלֹהֵי יַעֲקֹב

6. הָאֵל הַגָּדוֹל הַגִּבּוֹר וְהַנּוֹרָא, אֵל עֶלְיוֹן

Why do we need Hashem's help to pray?

1. גּוֹמֵל חֲסָדִים טוֹבִים, וְקֹנֵה הַכֹּל

2. וְזוֹכֵר חַסְדֵי אָבוֹת

3. וּמֵבִיא גוֹאֵל לִבְנֵי בְנֵיהֶם

4. לְמַעַן שְׁמוֹ בְּאַהֲבָה

These words are said between Rosh HaShana and Yom Kippur.

זָכְרֵנוּ לְחַיִּים, מֶלֶךְ חָפֵץ בְּחַיִּים
וְכָתְבֵנוּ בְּסֵפֶר הַחַיִּים, לְמַעַנְךָ אֱלֹהִים חַיִּים.

5. מֶלֶךְ עוֹזֵר וּמוֹשִׁיעַ וּמָגֵן.

6. בָּרוּךְ אַתָּה יהוה

7. מָגֵן אַבְרָהָם.

The Tefilla Text

Translation: *O* LORD, *open my lips, so that my mouth may declare Your praise.*

Blessed are You, LORD *our God and God of our fathers, God of Abraham, God of Isaac and God of Jacob; the great, mighty and awesome God, God Most High, who bestows acts of loving-kindness and creates all, who remembers the loving-kindness of the fathers and will bring a Redeemer to their children's children for the sake of His name, in love.*

[Between Rosh HaShana and Yom Kippur:]

Remember us for life, O King who desires life, and write us in the book of life – for Your sake, O God of life.

King, Helper, Savior, Shield: Blessed are You, LORD, *Shield of Abraham.*

The names of the *Avot* in the text are highlighted in colors that anchor them to the illustration. Avraham is highlighted in light brown and thereby linked to the tent in the illustration, Yitzḥak is highlighted in a deep brown and linked to the ram, and Yaakov is highlighted in orange, and linked to the ladder.

Special rubric icons are featured on this spread, to instruct the child on the choreography of this blessing in the *Amida*.

 Instructs the child to take three steps forward before they begin their *Amida*

 Instructs the child to bend their knees as they say the word ברוך

 Instructs the child to bow from the waist as they say the word אתה

Instructs the child to straighten to their full height when they say the name of Hashem

Educational Themes contained in the text:

- Before we even start we need to ask Hashem to help us to stand before Him and ask for our needs
- Standing on the shoulders of our *Avot* when we pray
- Transcendent God (הגדול הגבור והנורא, א-ל עליון) vs. immanent God (גומל חסדים, זוכר חסדי אבות, מלך עוזר ומושיע ומגן)
- Hashem as Protector
- The *Avot* taught us how and when to pray – they are the source of our *tefillot*

The Illustration

This illustration asks the child to connect to the characters of the *Avot* and their narratives, and reflect on the role they play on our *tefillot*. The illustration presents an abstract graphic representation of the three *Avot*, each one symbolized by an associated story and the values by which they are known. Avraham, represented here by a tent open wide, waiting to receive guests in fulfillment of the mitzva of הכנסת אורחים (welcoming guests into one's home), presents Avraham as a quintessential role model for kindness (חסד). Yitzḥak is represented by the ram that was sacrificed in his stead in the story of עקידת יצחק (the binding of Yitzḥak). Finally, Yaakov is represented by the ladder from the story of his dream.

Each of these personalities and concepts are intrinsically related to *tefilla*. We know that the Talmud (*Berakhot* 26b) explores the source of our three daily prayers services, *Shaḥarit*, *Minḥa* and *Ma'ariv*, and according to Rabbi Yossei the son of Rabbi Ḥanina, these three ser-

vices were instituted by Avraham, Yitzḥak, and Yaakov respectively. More than this, the concepts expressed in the images chosen to represent our forefathers are also central to *tefilla*. Avraham's ḥesed and concern for others is encapsulated in the communal nature of our prayers, and that they are voiced in the plural, consistently focusing on the entire nation rather than us as individuals. Yitzḥak as the sacrifice in the *Akeda* story embodies the relationship between the sacrificial service and the prayer service. Finally, Yaakov's ladder, as we have mentioned in the introduction, is considered as a metaphor for *tefilla* and the structure of *Tefillat Shaḥarit*, and is the inspiration for the navigation bar in this siddur.

Note that the fifth icon of the navigation bar is now highlighted (a person standing saying the *Amida*) signifying that we have entered the fifth section of the *Shaḥarit* service – the *Amida*.

The Kavana

Why do we need Hashem's help to pray?

This *kavana* asks the child to reflect on the natural difficulty that all humans encounter when praying to God. The very first sentence of this, the most impor-

tant *tefilla* (that is in fact just termed "*Tefilla*" in the Talmud to illustrate that point), pleads with Hashem to help us to open our mouths and to find the strength to ask for what we need, and find the meaning in the words to praise and thank Hashem sufficiently.

רפאנו
Refa'enu

The Tefilla Text

Translation: *Heal us, LORD, and we shall be healed. Save us and we shall be saved, for You are our praise. Bring complete recovery for all our ailments,*

[*Additional prayer for a sick person:*]

May it be Your will, O LORD my God and God of my ancestors, that You speedily send a complete recovery from heaven, a healing of both soul and body, to the patient (name), son/daughter of (mother's name) among the other afflicted of Israel.

for You, God, King, are a faithful and compassionate Healer. Blessed are You, LORD, Healer of the sick of His people Israel.

Educational Themes contained in the text:

- Humans (doctors) vs. God as primary healer (partnership!)
- Is health *the* most important blessing we ask for?
- Health = body *and* soul
- Praying for the collective and individuals

The Illustration

The illustration represents the concept of illness, and encourages the child to reflect on the role we play and the role Hashem plays in healing the sick. Dov is playing his part by visiting his friend who is sick in bed, fulfilling the mitzva of *bikkur ḥolim* (and has brought a balloon to cheer him up). The sick friend is holding a thermometer, and has medicine and hot cocoa on his bedside table. This represents the role that we play in healing the sick, versus the role Hashem plays, as represented by the text of the *tefilla*. The educator may wish to ask the children what they can do to help heal their sick friends, and the answers can be seen on the page of their siddur: pray to Hashem, *bikkur ḥolim*, medical help.

The Kavanot

The Upper *Kavana*: *How can you make sure you stay healthy?*

This *kavana* asks the child to reflect on illness prevention rather than curing illness, and explores the values of healthy living, our responsibility to look after ourselves, that our bodies and in fact life itself is a gift from God. This is an open question with no limit to the possibilities the children may arrive at.

The Lower *Kavana*: *"Our prayers are in the plural, because our prayers are not just for us here and now but for all the Jewish people… But we can say personal prayers, for example, for a sick relative, in this* ברכה."

This *kavana* is a paraphrased quote from Rabbi Adin Steinsaltz (in *A Guide to Jewish Prayer*, pp. 19–20) and asks the child to reflect on both the public and private nature of prayer, and how the entire *Amida* is voiced in the plural, demonstrating our concern for our entire nation and not just our own individual concerns. In fact, this addition to the *tefilla* for healing is the only *tefilla* in the *Amida* that gives us the chance to focus on an individual concern. And even this also speaks about *all* the sick among the Jewish people! The educator may wish to ask the children to brainstorm which issues and concerns are national and which are individual, and where and when we pray for them. Even the individual concerns can still be framed in a national context, such as this blessing for healing, and that is an important message.

שמע קולנו
Shema Kolenu

שְׁמַע קוֹלֵנוּ יהוה אֱלֹהֵינוּ

חוּס וְרַחֵם עָלֵינוּ

וְקַבֵּל בְּרַחֲמִים וּבְרָצוֹן אֶת תְּפִלָּתֵנוּ

כִּי אֵל שׁוֹמֵעַ תְּפִלּוֹת וְתַחֲנוּנִים אָתָּה

וּמִלְּפָנֶיךָ מַלְכֵּנוּ רֵיקָם אַל תְּשִׁיבֵנוּ

כִּי אַתָּה שׁוֹמֵעַ תְּפִלַּת עַמְּךָ יִשְׂרָאֵל

בְּרַחֲמִים.

בָּרוּךְ אַתָּה יהוה, שׁוֹמֵעַ תְּפִלָּה.

We ask Hashem to "listen" to our prayers rather than "answer" them. When is listening better than talking?

This בְּרָכָה is your chance to ask Hashem for anything you wish. What would you like to ask for today?

The Tefilla Text

Translation: *Listen to our voice,* LORD *our God. Spare us and have compassion on us, and in compassion and favor accept our prayer, for You, God, listen to prayers and pleas. Do not turn us away, O our King, empty-handed from Your presence, for You listen with compassion to the prayer of Your people Israel. Blessed are You,* LORD, *who listens to prayer.*

The words שומע תפלה are highlighted in olive green and anchored to the translation of those words in the upper *kavana*.

Educational Themes contained in the text:

- Personal prayers vs. collective prayers
- Hashem listens to our prayers because that is what He does (He is א-ל שומע תפלות)
- Asking God to accept our prayers with "compassion and favor" suggests that He should accept only the prayers that He thinks appropriate

The Illustration

This illustration asks the child to consider their *tefillot* soaring up to heaven to Hashem. The abstract concept of Hashem listening to our *tefillot* is somewhat challenging to represent pictorially. Here the illustration has Ellie and Dov climbing a mountain aspiring to reach the summit, and looking toward heaven. The mountain they are climbing is green and fertile (in contrast to the surrounding mountains), suggesting a place Hashem is concerned with and protective of. Here Hashem answers prayers. Ellie and Dov are yearning to connect to Hashem and get as close to Him as possible (the mountain's summit) or perhaps they themselves represent their *tefillot* as they climb toward heaven, closer and closer to Hashem.

The Kavanot

The Upper *Kavana*: *This* ברכה *is your chance to ask Hashem for anything you wish. What would you like to ask for today?*

This *kavana* encourages the child to feel empowered to ask Hashem for whatever their heart desires. This should help to foster a connection with Hashem, and an understanding that Hashem is the source of all blessings in our lives, and the address for prayers. This *kavana* can be explored everyday (and certainly on multiple occasions) as the answer could (and should!) be different each day. The educator could use this opportunity to explain that this is a general blessing for the acceptance of *tefillot* and therefore a place where we allow any requests in any language to be inserted.

The Lower *Kavana*: *We ask Hashem to "listen" to our prayers rather than "answer" them. When is listening better than talking?*

This *kavana* asks the child to reflect on the language of שומע תפלה – why don't we say that Hashem answers our prayers? Why is it good to know He listens even if we don't get a response? We are declaring that although Hashem may choose not to answer in the affirmative to our requests and *tefillot*, it is comforting to know He is always listening and considering our lives for our benefit. Rabbi J.B. Soloveitchik gives an example of this from his own life. He fervently prayed for circumstances that would have allowed him to remain in Europe in 1932 rather than immigrate to America. God, in His compassion, did not accept his prayer. But He was certainly listening! The second half of the *kavana* asks the child to understand the importance of listening to the people in our lives (and of being listened to). Sometimes people just need to know you are listening and are not asking to hear what you think. Listening is not the absence of something. It is an act in itself.

מודים 1
Modim 1

The Tefilla Text

Translation: *We give thanks to You, for You are the LORD our God and God of our ancestors for ever and all time. You are the Rock of our lives, Shield of our salvation from generation to generation. We will thank You and declare Your praise for our lives, which are entrusted into Your hand; for our souls, which are placed in Your charge; for Your miracles which are with us every day; and for Your wonders and favors at all times, evening, morning and midday. You are good – for Your compassion never fails. You are compassionate – for Your loving kindnesses never cease. We have always placed our hope in You.*

The word מודים is highlighted in brown and anchored to the word "thank" in the lower *kavana*.

Educational Themes contained in the text:

- Thanksgiving
- Bowing = physical act of subservience and admission of dependence
- Miracles = extraordinary events that are universally recognized as an act of God

- Wonders = happen every day and run the risk of being taken for granted

The Illustration

This illustration is instructional, and has Ellie praying the *Amida* prayer from her siddur. She has reached the *Modim* blessing, and is demonstrating that one must bow from the waist at the word *Modim*. This is also indicated by the icon that accompanies the rubric. The upper *kavana* on the page explores the emotional experience of bowing and its relevance to this blessing.

The Kavanot

The Upper *Kavana: Why do people bow? How do you feel when you bow?*

This question asks the child to reflect on the emotional experience of bowing in front of a person or power, and how the mechanics of bowing is conducive to that appropriate emotion. This should then be related to the experience of bowing in front of Hashem during the process of thanking Him for what He does for us. There are many cultures that use bowing as a means of showing respect, such as Far-Eastern societies, and the subjects of European royalty. The act of bowing shows respect, subservience and contrition. This is an appropriate emotion to encourage ourselves to experience when saying a blessing that thanks (and thereby acknowledges) Hashem as the source of all blessing in our lives. The educator may wish to ask the children to carry out practical demonstrations of bowing in other situations (such as business meetings in Japan, a kung fu fight in China, or meeting the Queen of England) and ask the children to describe how it feels to bow in these situations. The children can then be asked why the Rabbis decided this was an appropriate action to signal the beginning of this blessing (and why none of the other blessings)?

The Lower *Kavana: What would you like to thank Hashem for today?*

Parallel to the lower *kavana* on the previous page (*Shema Kolenu*) where the children were encouraged to ask Hashem for whatever they liked, this *kavana* directs the child to thank Hashem for whatever they believe they should. This is intended to provide the child with a sense of empowerment and ownership of their prayers, as they analyze their own lives to decide what they need to thank Hashem for. This should help to foster a connection with Hashem, and an understanding that Hashem is the source of all blessings in our lives, and the address for prayers. This *kavana* can be explored everyday (and certainly on multiple occasions) as the answer could (and should) be different each day.

מודים 2
Modim 2

The Tefilla Text

Translation: [On Ḥanukka and Purim:]

[We thank You also] for the miracles, the redemption, the mighty deeds, the salvations, and the victories in battle which You performed for our ancestors in those days, at this time.

For all these things may Your name be blessed and exalted, our King, continually, for ever and all time.

[Between Rosh HaShana and Yom Kippur:]

And write, for a good life, all the children of Your covenant.

Let all that lives thank You, Selah! and praise Your name in truth, God, our Savior and Help, Selah! Blessed are You, LORD, whose name is "the Good" and to whom thanks are due.

The words על הנסים are highlighted in orange and anchored to the upper *kavana*, and the word הטוב is highlighted in green and anchored to the words "The Good" in the lower *kavana*.

Educational Themes contained in the text:

- Miracles – the interplay between our role and the role of God

- Miracles through nature and supernatural miracles
- The God of History – Divine Providence/*Hashgaha*
- *"In those days, at this time"* – Historical national miracles as a template for modern national miracles

The Illustration

This illustration focuses on the festivals on which *Al HaNissim* is said as days of miracles and thanksgiving, and subtly equates them with the modern-day equivalent – the establishment of the State of Israel and all the miracles of modern Jewish history associated with Israel. The illustration encourages the child to reflect on Ḥanukka and Purim as days of thanksgiving to Hashem, and although we do not say *Al HaNissim* on Yom HaAtzma'ut, we are asking the children to see this day also as a day of celebration and thanksgiving for the miracles Hashem has performed throughout the history of the State of Israel. The illustration references Ḥanukka in the *menora*, Purim in the *megilla*, and Israel in the flag of the State of Israel seen in the background. Note the blue bands in the flag that is blowing in the gentle wind, as well as the *Magen David*. The blue bands on the flag of the State of Israel were chosen to remind us of the stripes found on the *tallit*, and the color blue was chosen to remind us of the *tekhelet* of the mitzva of *tzitzit*. The children could explore why the founding fathers of the State of Israel decided to incorporate these themes in the national symbols they chose.

The Kavanot

The Upper *Kavana*: *How does Hashem make miracles in your life?*

This *kavana* asks the child to reflect on the impact of Hashem in their lives, and connect to Hashem as an ever-present force in their lives. The question implies that there are miracles in everyone's life, and it is just a matter of identifying them. The educator may wish to begin by defining miracles, and guiding the children to realize that God can guide our lives through nature and through supernatural means, and both can be defined as miraculous. Once the child has absorbed this idea, they should be ready to explore the role of Hashem in their lives, both in a personal way (*hashgaha peratit*), and perhaps they may also be able to talk about Hashem's impact on the world in general (*hashgaha kelalit*).

The Lower *Kavana*: *Why do you think Hashem is called "The Good"?*

This *kavana* asks the children to connect to the definition of God as "Good." When we describe God as good in the context of this blessing, which concentrates on the things we need to thank Him for, including His role in history (with explicit examples in the form of the addition *Al HaNissim*), we are declaring our belief that everything God does is for the good, even if we cannot always understand it, and even if it does not seem that way from our perspective. These are complex philosophical ideas that can still be understood on an appropriate level for this developmental age. The educator may wish to use the mosaic metaphor (perhaps in a practical way asking the children to create their own mosaic) – when you only look at a small section of a mosaic it is hard to make out any order, but if you take a step back and see the larger picture it all makes sense (the back of a tapestry also works for this, and can also be used in a practical way for children to experience). Both *kavanot* on this page can be combined to focus on real-world examples from the children's lives.

שים שלום
Sim Shalom

The Tefilla Text

Translation: *Grant peace, goodness and blessing, grace, loving-kindness and compassion to us and all Israel Your people. Bless us, our Father, all as one, with the light of Your face, for by the light of Your face You have given us, LORD our God, the Torah of life and love of kindness, righteousness, blessing, compassion, life and peace. May it be good in Your eyes to bless Your people Israel at every time, in every hour, with Your peace.*

[Between Rosh HaShana and Yom Kippur:]

In the book of life, blessing, peace and prosperity, may we and all Your people the house of Israel be remembered and written before You for a good life, and for peace.

Blessed are You, LORD, who blesses His people Israel with peace.

The words שים שלום and תורת חיים are highlighted in brown, anchoring them to the *kavana*, as well as to the illustration (the tree).

Educational Themes contained in the text:

- "Bless us as one" = peace can only be established when there is true equality of people. These are the values upon which peace will be established: grace; loving-kindness; compassion; [values of] life.

- The relationship between the Torah, and ḥesed, and peace
- Peace is the ultimate hope of Judaism and therefore the way the ultimate prayer concludes.
- A tranquil conclusion to a *tefilla* of emotional highs and lows (love, fear, mercy, forgiveness, helplessness, yearning, redemption, etc.).

The Illustration

The illustration encourages the children to reflect on the relationship between our behavior and our values and the achievement of peace in our world. The text of this *tefilla* juxtaposes peace, goodness and blessing, grace, loving-kindness and compassion, and places them under the umbrella category of peace (by beginning and concluding the blessing with the value of peace). The blessing suggests that these values have been given to us by God in His *Torat Ḥayyim*, and we ask Him to ensure that our world is full of them.

In the illustration we see Dov climbing a tree in order to shoo away the mother bird (a dove, who represents peace, and is featured in the following page spread also) before taking the eggs from the nest. This is the mitzva of *shiluaḥ haken* (שילוח הקן) which we learn about in *Devarim* 22:6–7. While some would interpret this

mitzva as showing concern for animal welfare, Rambam, in his *Guide for the Perplexed* (3:27), presents all mitzvot as designed to benefit man – either to benefit their body or to benefit their soul. Rambam believes that mitzvot such as *sheḥita* and *shiluaḥ haken* are less about showing mercy and concern for animals and more about training man to know how to interact with his fellow man and how to create a just society. The illustration is suggesting that the value of ḥesed, as learnt from the mitzva of *shiluaḥ haken*, is central to building a society on the foundation of peace.

The educator may wish to explore with the children how peace can be achieved. What do we need to make sure happens in our classroom to ensure that there is peace? How can the Torah help us to do this?

The Kavana

"The Torah's ways are pleasant and all its paths lead to peace."

This *kavana* asks the children to reflect on how the Torah and the mitzvot can lead to peace between us and our friends, and how we can use the things we learn in the Torah to build a peaceful society (for the children that would be the group interactions within the classroom). This *kavana* is a quote from *Mishlei* 3:17, which is quoted in the well-known midrash: "Everything written in the Torah was written for the sake of peace" (*Tanḥuma, Tzav* 3). This presents peace as a meta-value, toward which the whole of the Torah

is driven. However, it also highlights our responsibility to create peace. We cannot just sit back and pray for God to bring peace to the world, the Torah is focused on our responsibility to create a peaceful society and to behave in a way to our fellow man that will best achieve peace. Peace will be achieved through a partnership between man and God. We must do our part. This is also explored in the *kavana* on the following page.

The educator may wish to ask the children to give examples of mitzvot that can "lead to peace" and perhaps give some less obvious examples, such as Shabbat, *hashavat aveda* (returning lost property), or *shemitta*.

עושה שלום
Oseh Shalom

The Tefilla Text

Translation: *May He who makes peace in His high places, make peace for us and all Israel – and say: Amen.*

The words הוא יעשה שלום are highlighted in orange and anchored to the upper *kavana*.

Special rubric icons are featured on this spread, to instruct the child on the choreography of this final part of the *Amida*.

Instructs the child to bow as they take three steps backwards at the conclusion of the *Amida*

Instructs the child to bow toward the left as they say the words עושה שלום במרומיו

Instructs the child to bow toward the right as they say the words הוא יעשה שלום

Instructs the child to bow forward from the waist as they say the words עלינו ועל כל ישראל

It should be noted that the figure in the icons is deliberately depicted bowing in the opposite direction to the instruction, as in a mirror image, in recognition of a child's natural response to mirror actions. This will encourage the child to bow in the correct direction.

Educational Themes contained in the text:

- Peace on High (Heaven) and peace below on earth
- Peace is the ultimate hope of Judaism and therefore the way the ultimate prayer concludes.
- A tranquil conclusion to a *tefilla* of emotional highs and lows (love, mercy, dread, helplessness, yearning, confusion, terror.
- Where in the world are there Jews most in need of peace?

The Illustration

This illustration presents a peaceful scene for the children to reflect on the tranquil nature of peace. In the illustration Dov and a friend are out in nature enjoying a peaceful walk when they spot a dove, and enjoy its beauty and significance. The white dove is traditionally seen as a symbol of peace. This comes from the story of Noaḥ and the flood. At the conclusion of the flood Noaḥ let a dove fly free to determine if the waters were abating. The dove returned to him with an olive branch (also a symbol of peace for the same reason) to demonstrate that the waters were in fact receding, and the world was entering a new peaceful age after the destruction of the flood.

The Kavanot

The Upper *Kavana: How will you partner with Hashem to make peace in the world?*

As we explore on the previous page, we have a responsibility to partner with Hashem in bringing peace into our lives and into the world. This question asks the child to reflect on how, in practical concrete terms, they plan to do this.

The Lower *Kavana: "Hillel says: Be among the students of Aaron, loving peace and chasing peace, loving people, and bringing them closer to the Torah."*

This *kavana* is the famous mishna in the Ethics of the Fathers (*Pirkei Avot* 1:12) that encourages us to see Aaron as a role model for peace. Not only did he love peace, but he actively pursued it, once again reaffirming our responsibility to create peace in the world, rather than merely praying to Hashem to do the job for us. Aaron was a peace maker, actively working to achieve peace in his life and among the people that surrounded him. He did this because he was a lover of all people, and that is the telling value that underlies those that want to create peace in the world. But the mishna does not stop there. It gives us a very practical way to achieve the goals that Aaron became famous for. We should bring people closer to the Torah and the values contained therein. Just as we discovered on the previous page, the values of Torah are the vehicle to bring peace in the world.

אבינו מלכנו
Avinu Malkenu

In what ways is
Hashem like a parent?

This תְּפִלָּה is said on fast days and between
Rosh HaShana and Yom Kippur.

אָבִינוּ מַלְכֵּנוּ, חָנֵּנוּ וַעֲנֵנוּ

כִּי אֵין בָּנוּ מַעֲשִׂים

עֲשֵׂה עִמָּנוּ צְדָקָה וָחֶסֶד

וְהוֹשִׁיעֵנוּ.

It once happened that
no rain had fallen.
Rabbi Akiva prayed
with the words:
"Our Father, our King,
we have no King but You,"
and the rains then fell.

The Tefilla Text

Translation: *Our Father, our King, be gracious to us and answer us, though we have no worthy deeds; act with us in charity and loving-kindness and save us.*

The word אבינו is highlighted in green and anchored to the upper *kavana*.

Educational Themes contained in the text:

- God as King (Justice, power, demands obedience)
- God as Parent/Father (love, compassion, forgiveness, intimacy)
- Source of this prayer = a story from Rabbi Akiva's life

The Illustration

This illustration depicts the story behind the origins of this *tefilla*, as found in the Talmud (*Ta'anit* 25b) and paraphrased in the lower *kavana* on this page. Here is the story in the original:

It is related of Rabbi Eliezer that he once stepped before the Ark [to lead the congregation in prayer] and recited the twenty-four benedictions [of the Amida for fast days declared on account of drought], and his prayer was not answered. Rabbi Akiva stepped before the Ark after him and exclaimed: "Our Father, our King! We have no king but You! Our Father, our King! For Your sake, have compassion for us!" And rain fell.

Rabbi Akiva stands on the parched dry ground with his arms outstretched to the heavens crying out to Hashem for rain for the people. We can see the rain-clouds gathering as Rabbi Akiva's *tefillot* are answered. Note the presence of Ellie and Dov in the illustration (or their Talmudic ancestors), and the adults who have brought their vessels to catch the rain that is bound to fall because they have such faith in Hashem and/or the power of Rabbi Akiva's prayer. This could be used by the educator to discuss what faith and belief is. The educator should also consider exploring with the children why this *tefilla* is said on fast days and between Rosh HaShana and Yom Kippur. What is the relationship between this story and these times? Why would this *tefilla* be an appropriate way to approach Hashem on these days?

The Kavanot

The Upper *Kavana: In what ways is Hashem like a parent?*

This *kavana* asks the child to connect to Hashem in the role of Parent. At various times in this siddur we have asked the child to consider God as a King (such as *Adon Olam* and *Aleinu*), and this *tefilla* also presents to us a model of connection to God in the role of King. But it is God as Parent that we are here asking the children to reflect on. The educator could ask the children what similarities there are between a parent and Hashem (such as love, protection, creation, etc.) as well as asking them to consider the contrast between Hashem as Parent and Hashem as King.

The Lower *Kavana: It once happened that no rain had fallen. Rabbi Akiva prayed with the words: "Our Father, our King, we have no King but You," and the rains then fell.*

This is the paraphrased story from the Talmud (*Ta'anit* 25b), the historical source for this *tefilla*. The implication of the story is that it was the formula, "Our Father, Our King," that forced God's hand to give the people rain. When we remind Hashem (or remind ourselves) that we have an intimate relationship of love with Hashem as well as a respectful reverence toward Him as King, then He is ready to take His responsibility as our Protector and Sustainer (responsibilities of both a father and a king) to the next level.

ויהי בנסע
VaYehi Binsoa

These verses are said on days when the סֵפֶר תּוֹרָה is taken from the אֲרוֹן קֹדֶשׁ and read.

Why do you think we read from the Torah when we are together in the בֵּית כְּנֶסֶת?

1 וַיְהִי בִּנְסֹעַ הָאָרֹן וַיֹּאמֶר מֹשֶׁה
2 קוּמָה יהוה וְיָפֻצוּ אֹיְבֶיךָ וְיָנֻסוּ
3 מְשַׂנְאֶיךָ מִפָּנֶיךָ: כִּי מִצִּיּוֹן תֵּצֵא
4 תוֹרָה וּדְבַר־יהוה מִירוּשָׁלָ͏ִם:
5 בָּרוּךְ שֶׁנָּתַן תּוֹרָה לְעַמּוֹ יִשְׂרָאֵל
6 בִּקְדֻשָּׁתוֹ.

"Jerusalem will become a torch for the nations of the world who will walk by its light."

The Tefilla Text

Translation: *Whenever the Ark set out, Moses would say, "Arise, LORD, and may Your enemies be scattered. May those who hate You flee before You." For the Torah shall come forth from Zion, and the word of the LORD from Jerusalem. Blessed is He who in His holiness gave the Torah to His people Israel.*

The words כי מציון תצא תורה ודבר ה׳ מירושלם are highlighted in brown and anchored to the lower *kavana*.

Educational Themes contained in the text:

- Public Torah reading = A reenactment of the revelation at Sinai
- Prayer = speaking; *Keriat HaTorah* = listening
- *Aron HaKodesh* (its role in our synagogue or in the *Beit HaMikdash/Mishkan*)
- Jerusalem (Torah emanating from Israel today)

The Illustration

The illustration encourages the children to reflect on the connection between the public reading of the Torah in synagogue today to the historical and spiritual experience of the giving of the Torah on Mount Sinai. Dov is reading from the Torah which rests on the *shulḥan*, presumably in the synagogue, while holding the *yad* to point to the words. In the background our characters are waiting at the foot of Mount Sinai to receive the Torah. Note the path to the summit where the tablets of stone await the Children of Israel is stepped, showing easy access. The receiving of the Torah was not a one-time event limited to one generation only. The Torah and the spiritual experience of receiving it, is available for us every time there is a public reading.

The tablets of stone , resting at the summit of Mount Sinai, represent the actual giving of the Torah from Hashem to Moshe, shown here in their traditional form, rather than the arched shape that Christian sources have made famous. Again, Ellie or her ancestor, is present in this scene, directly referencing the midrash that suggests all of our *neshamot* were present at that time. This should encourage us all to feel connected to this event, to the reading of the Torah ceremony in synagogue, and to the *Sefer Torah* itself. While it is Dov who is reading from the Torah, Ellie is found in the depiction of the historical event of the receiving of the Torah, encouraging both boys and girls to feel connected to this event, and to the Torah itself.

The Kavanot

The Upper *Kavana*: *Why do you think we read from the Torah when we are together in the* בית כנסת*?*

This *kavana*, which is colored in brown to anchor it to the *shulḥan* from which Dov is reading the Torah, asks the child to reflect on the experience of public Torah reading, and to connect to the *Sefer Torah* as a part of that. It is an open question with no incorrect answers. Answers that the children (or educator) may suggest could include:

- To inspire the congregation
- For those that wouldn't have the chance (or ability) to learn Torah themselves
- To bring the community together
- To reenact the Receiving of the Torah
- To allow us to see and touch the *Sefer Torah*
- To give Hashem a chance to talk to us (we have had our turn in our *tefillot*)

The Lower *Kavana*: *"Jerusalem will become a torch for the nations of the world who will walk by its light."*

This *kavana*, a quote from the Midrash (*Yalkut Shimoni, Yishayahu* 499), asks the child to reflect on the verse כי מציון תצא תורה ודבר ה׳ מירושלם and its meaning. The Midrash suggests that Jerusalem, and all that it represents, will light the world, helping them to see through the darkness. With the help of the verse (*Yishayahu* 2:3) highlighted in red in the *tefilla* and linked to this corresponding *kavana*, we can understand that Torah, and the People of Israel, in the Land of Israel, will bring light and wisdom to the world, through demonstrating how to live and serve God. The context of this verse is a Messianic vision for the end of days. When we as a people manage to live as a model nation, then the world will be ready for Messianic times. The educator may wish to explore the notion of being a chosen people, the concept of role modeling, and what "light" might mean to the world.

עלינו
Aleinu

The Tefilla Text

Translation: *It is our duty to praise the Master of all, and ascribe greatness to the Author of creation.*

As it is written in Your Torah: "The LORD will reign for ever and ever." And it is said: "Then the LORD shall be King over all the earth; on that day the LORD shall be One and His name One."

The words והיה ה׳ למלך על כל הארץ is highlighted in green and anchored to both the upper *kavana* (on the left of the page) as well as the words "Hashem is King" in the lower (right-hand) *kavana*.

Educational Themes contained in the text:

- *Malkhut* – God as King of the Universe
- One day, in Messianic times, all will acknowledge God

The Illustration

This illustration asks the child to reflect on God as King of the Universe, and that one day He will be accepted as such by the entire world. This time will be when the Messiah comes. In the illustration, Dov and Ellie, together with all of their friends, are building a crown for Hashem, declaring Him as King, with bricks from Jerusalem. Jerusalem represents Messianic times, when all Jews will have returned to the Land of Israel and there will be a Temple built there. This is the time when all of the world will accept Hashem as King of the Universe. It is not by chance that this illustration includes not only Dov and Ellie, but also their friends, their community, because it takes community and society to bring the Messiah. When we learn to treat each other with respect and love and build a society based on those values, only then will there be a time when the world is ready to accept Hashem as Sovereign, and usher in Messianic times.

The Kavanot

The Upper *Kavana*: *"One day Hashem will be accepted as King over the entire world."*

This *kavana* asks the child to reflect on what it would take for Hashem to be accepted by the entire world as King of the Universe. It is a paraphrased translation from the verse והיה ה׳ למלך על כל הארץ in the text of the *tefilla*. The educator may wish to use this as an opportunity to explore what the Messiah means and what Messianic times might be. What might it take to bring the Messiah to the world?

The Lower *Kavana*: *How can we show that Hashem is King?*

This *kavana* asks the child to connect to Hashem as King of the Universe, and to reflect on how we can relate to Him in this way. The educator may wish to brainstorm with the children what a king is, what a king does, and how we should interact with a king. What powers does a king have and what responsibilities to us as his subjects? What are the differences between an earthly king and the King of kings? The educator may wish to connect this page with *Avinu Malkenu* where Hashem is described as not only a King, but also as a Parent. As *Avinu Malkenu* is rarely said, this could be a more appropriate time to reflect on the differences between these two ways to relate to Hashem. Some of these themes have also been explored earlier on the *Adon Olam* spread on p. 25.

הדלקת נרות שבת
Lighting Shabbat Candles

On Friday night we say this בְּרָכָה before we light the Shabbat candles.

Shabbat candles **give light and warmth to our homes. What will you give this Shabbat?**

1 בָּרוּךְ אַתָּה יהוה
2 אֱלֹהֵינוּ מֶלֶךְ הָעוֹלָם
3 אֲשֶׁר קִדְּשָׁנוּ בְּמִצְוֹתָיו וְצִוָּנוּ
4 לְהַדְלִיק נֵר שֶׁל שַׁבָּת.

The candles show that Shabbat is special. How will you show that Shabbat is special?

The Tefilla Text

Translation: *Blessed are You,* LORD *our God, King of the Universe, who has made us holy through His commandments, and has commanded us to light the Sabbath light.*

The words נר של שבת are highlighted in orange and anchored to the words "Shabbat candles" in the upper *kavana*, and to the flames of the Shabbat candles in the illustration.

Educational Themes contained in the text:

- *Shalom bayit*
- The light of the Shabbat candles and their impact
- The Jewish mother

The Illustration

This illustration asks the children to reflect on the tranquility of Shabbat and the how the Shabbat candles can contribute to that. We join Ellie and Dov in the home at the beginning of Shabbat, and meet their mother once again (we will be in their home again during Shabbat and meet their father as well!). From the illustration we can see how this ritual can be a wonderful opportunity for a family experience and the relationship between the children and their mother is portrayed here. The importance and impact of Shabbat clothing is also highlighted here (look how beautiful the children look in their *bigdei Shabbat*!), and how the candles seem to give the room and the scene a special light. Note that the mother lights the big pair of candles, and Ellie lights the small pair. Some families have the custom to light a candle for each member of the family. Some have the custom for each girl to light her own candle (or two candles) in addition to the mother's candles. Our family here combines the two customs, lighting four candles, one for each member of the family. Ellie lights the small candles, while their mother lights the big candles.

Note that navigation bar has been exchanged for four new icons. The first of them, Shabbat candles, indicates the section for the Shabbat Evening.

The Kavanot

The Upper *Kavana: Shabbat candles give light and warmth to our homes. What will you give this Shabbat?*

This *kavana* asks the children to reflect on the role and impact of the Shabbat candles, and how they can bring *shalom bayit* – peace in the home. The candles literally bring light and warmth, but can also be a figurative representation of *shalom bayit*. The children are asked to compare themselves to Shabbat candles, and to think about how they can also bring *shalom bayit* into their homes. Just as the warmth and light of the candles bring *shalom* into the home, so the children can bring *shalom* and a special Shabbat atmosphere into their homes. This could be from good behavior, from helping their parents on Shabbat, from attending synagogue, from singing *zemirot*, or from sharing what they learned at school that week at the Shabbat table.

The Lower *Kavana: The candles show that Shabbat is special. How will you show that Shabbat is special?*

This *kavana* asks the children to reflect on the ways that we make Shabbat special. We begin Shabbat with special candles, and we have many opportunities throughout Shabbat to demonstrate to ourselves, to others, and to Hashem, that Shabbat is special. These include the way we dress, the food we eat, the activities we do with our friends and family, and the things we read and learn (reference can be made to the beautiful Shabbat clothes we see Dov and Ellie wearing in the illustration, and the special white Shabbat tablecloth on the table). The word "special" in this *kavana* is hinting at the Hebrew word עונג, which is often used in the context of Shabbat, or כבוד which often is used to refer to preparation for Shabbat and the things we dedicate to Shabbat to make it special. We learn the concept of כבוד שבת and עונג שבת from the verse in *Yishayahu*:

אִם-תָּשִׁיב מִשַּׁבָּת רַגְלֶךָ, עֲשׂוֹת חֲפָצֶךָ בְּיוֹם קָדְשִׁי; וְקָרָאתָ לַשַּׁבָּת עֹנֶג, לִקְדוֹשׁ יְהוָה מְכֻבָּד, וְכִבַּדְתּוֹ מֵעֲשׂוֹת דְּרָכֶיךָ, מִמְּצוֹא חֶפְצְךָ וְדַבֵּר דָּבָר.

If you turn away your foot because of the Sabbath, from pursuing your business on My holy day; and call the Sabbath a delight, and the holy of the LORD *honorable; and honor it, not doing your wonted ways, nor pursuing your business, nor speaking thereof. (Yishayahu 58:13–14)*

לכה דודי 1
Lekha Dodi 1

73

מְקַדֵּשׁ מֶלֶךְ עִיר מְלוּכָה 1
קוּמִי צְאִי מִתּוֹךְ הַהֲפֵכָה 2
רַב לָךְ שֶׁבֶת בְּעֵמֶק הַבָּכָא 3
וְהוּא יַחֲמֹל עָלַיִךְ חֶמְלָה. 4
לְכָה דוֹדִי לִקְרַאת כַּלָּה, פְּנֵי שַׁבָּת נְקַבְּלָה. 5

הִתְנַעֲרִי, מֵעָפָר קוּמִי 6
לִבְשִׁי בִּגְדֵי תִפְאַרְתֵּךְ עַמִּי 7
עַל יַד בֶּן יִשַׁי בֵּית הַלַּחְמִי 8
קָרְבָה אֶל נַפְשִׁי, גְאָלָהּ. 9
לְכָה דוֹדִי לִקְרַאת כַּלָּה, פְּנֵי שַׁבָּת נְקַבְּלָה. 10

הִתְעוֹרְרִי הִתְעוֹרְרִי 11
כִּי בָא אוֹרֵךְ קוּמִי אוֹרִי 12
עוּרִי עוּרִי, שִׁיר דַּבֵּרִי 13
כְּבוֹד יהוה עָלַיִךְ נִגְלָה. 14
לְכָה דוֹדִי לִקְרַאת כַּלָּה, פְּנֵי שַׁבָּת נְקַבְּלָה. 15

72

This special song is sung on Friday night to begin Shabbat.

לְכָה דוֹדִי לִקְרַאת כַּלָּה, פְּנֵי שַׁבָּת נְקַבְּלָה. 1
לְכָה דוֹדִי לִקְרַאת כַּלָּה, פְּנֵי שַׁבָּת נְקַבְּלָה. 2

שָׁמוֹר וְזָכוֹר בְּדִבּוּר אֶחָד 3
הִשְׁמִיעָנוּ אֵל הַמְיֻחָד 4
יהוה אֶחָד וּשְׁמוֹ אֶחָד 5
לְשֵׁם וּלְתִפְאֶרֶת וְלִתְהִלָּה. 6
לְכָה דוֹדִי לִקְרַאת כַּלָּה, פְּנֵי שַׁבָּת נְקַבְּלָה. 7

לִקְרַאת שַׁבָּת לְכוּ וְנֵלְכָה 8
כִּי הִיא מְקוֹר הַבְּרָכָה 9
מֵרֹאשׁ מִקֶּדֶם נְסוּכָה 10
סוֹף מַעֲשֶׂה בְּמַחֲשָׁבָה תְחִלָּה. 11
לְכָה דוֹדִי לִקְרַאת כַּלָּה, פְּנֵי שַׁבָּת נְקַבְּלָה. 12

The Rabbis of Tzefat would sing לְכָה דוֹדִי as they went out into the fields as the sun was setting, to welcome the Shabbat Bride.

The Tefilla Text

Translation: *Come, my Beloved, to greet the bride; let us welcome the Sabbath. Come, my Beloved, to greet the bride; let us welcome the Sabbath.*

"Observe" and "Remember" in one act of speech, the One and Only God made us hear. The LORD is One and His name is One, for renown, for splendor, and for praise.

To greet the Sabbath, come let us go, for of blessing, she is the source. From the outset, as of old, ordained: Last in deed, first in thought.

Sanctuary of the King, royal city, arise, go forth from your ruined state. Too long have you dwelt in the valley of tears. He will shower compassion on you.

Shake yourself off, arise from the dust! Put on your clothes of glory, My people. Through the son of Jesse the Bethlehemite, Draw near to my soul and redeem it.

Wake up, wake up, For your light has come: rise, shine! Awake, awake, break out in song, For the LORD's glory is revealed on you.

The words לקראת כלה are highlighted in orange and anchored to the words "to welcome the Shabbat Bride" in the lower *kavana*.

Educational Themes contained in the text:

- Shabbat as a bride and Shabbat as a queen
- Shabbat observance (positive mitzvot vs. negative mitzvot)
- Shabbat in the Ten Commandments
- Shabbat themes: blessing; light; song; "clothes of glory"

The Illustration

This illustration, as well as the corresponding illustration on the following page where Lekha Dodi continues, portrays the famous story of the kabbalists of Tzefat in the sixteenth century, who would go into the fields in the hills surrounding this holy city in *Eretz Yisrael* and, singing this *tefilla*, would greet and welcome Shabbat as if Shabbat was a beautiful bride entering the *ḥupa*. We see the homes of Tzefat perched on a hillside on the right-hand side, with the majority of the page taken up with a symbolic and serene blue-and-white background, encouraging the child to feel the spiritual and tranquil nature of Shabbat. On the left-hand side of the page musical notes are found, suggesting the importance of music and song in Judaism, Shabbat, and this *tefilla* in particular.

The Kavana

The Rabbis of Tzefat would sing לכה דודי *as they went out into the fields as the sun was setting, to welcome the Shabbat Bride.*

This *kavana* tells the story of the kabbalists of Tzefat who would go into the fields in the hills surrounding Tzefat singing this *tefilla* to greet and welcome Shabbat. The educator may wish to use this as an opportunity to explore the similarities between Shabbat and a bride, and why we relate to Shabbat in this way.

לכה דודי 2
Lekha Dodi 2

<table>
<tr><td>

75

1 וְהָיוּ לִמְשִׁסָּה שֹאסָיִךְ
2 וְרָחֲקוּ כָּל מְבַלְּעָיִךְ
3 יָשִׂישׂ עָלַיִךְ אֱלֹהָיִךְ
4 כִּמְשׂושׂ חָתָן עַל כַּלָּה.
5 לְכָה דוֹדִי לִקְרַאת כַּלָּה, פְּנֵי שַׁבָּת נְקַבְּלָה.

6 יָמִין וּשְׂמֹאל תִּפְרֹצִי
7 וְאֶת יהוה תַּעֲרִיצִי
8 עַל יַד אִישׁ בֶּן פַּרְצִי
9 וְנִשְׂמְחָה וְנָגִילָה.
10 לְכָה דוֹדִי לִקְרַאת כַּלָּה, פְּנֵי שַׁבָּת נְקַבְּלָה.

At this point we turn to face the back of the בֵּית כְּנֶסֶת as we welcome the bride – Shabbat. Bow to greet her at the words בּוֹאִי כַלָּה and then turn to face forward.

11 בּוֹאִי בְשָׁלוֹם עֲטֶרֶת בַּעְלָהּ
12 גַּם בְּשִׂמְחָה וּבְצָהֳלָה
13 תּוֹךְ אֱמוּנֵי עַם סְגֻלָּה
14 בּוֹאִי כַלָּה, בּוֹאִי כַלָּה.
15 לְכָה דוֹדִי לִקְרַאת כַּלָּה, פְּנֵי שַׁבָּת נְקַבְּלָה.

</td><td>

74

1 לֹא תֵבֹשִׁי וְלֹא תִכָּלְמִי
2 מַה תִּשְׁתּוֹחֲחִי וּמַה תֶּהֱמִי
3 בָּךְ יֶחֱסוּ עֲנִיֵּי עַמִּי
4 וְנִבְנְתָה עִיר עַל תִּלָּהּ.
5 לְכָה דוֹדִי לִקְרַאת כַּלָּה, פְּנֵי שַׁבָּת נְקַבְּלָה.

Have you ever seen a beautiful sunset? What do you think of when you see beauty in nature?

</td></tr>
</table>

The Tefilla Text

Translation: *Do not be ashamed, do not be confounded. Why be downcast? Why do you mourn? In you the needy of My people find shelter, and the city shall be rebuilt on its hill.*

Come, my Beloved, to greet the bride; let us welcome the Sabbath.

Those who despoiled you shall be despoiled, and all who devoured you shall be far away. Your God will rejoice over you as a bridegroom rejoices over his bride.

Right and left you shall spread out, and God you will revere. Through the descendant of Peretz, we shall rejoice and we shall be glad.

Come in peace, O crown of her husband; come with joy and jubilation, among the faithful of the treasured people. Enter, O bride! Enter, O bride!

Educational Themes contained in the text:

- Shabbat as a bride and Shabbat as a queen
- Hashem = groom; Israel = bride
- Happiness and joy
- Shabbat and peace
- *Am segula*

The Illustration

This illustration continues the story of the kabbalists of Tzefat from the previous page. Here we see the kabbalists leaving the old holy city of Tzefat in the background, gazing out across the hills to the sunset, as they sing with their souls this beautiful song to welcome Shabbat. Notice the change in the colors and texture of the sky as the illustration draws the child's attention to the setting sun, and the colors that are reflected in the sky from that.

The Kavana

Have you ever seen a beautiful sunset? What do you think of when you see beauty in nature?

This *kavana* asks the child to reflect on the beauty contained in nature all around them, and to connect to Hashem through that. The Rabbis of Tzefat have embraced the spiritual essence of nature, and use it weekly to achieve a spiritual high as Shabbat begins. Through gazing at the sunset from the magnificent hills surrounding their homes, they see and sense God as they welcome this spiritual day into their hearts. By asking the children to reflect on their own experience of nature, we are encouraging them to do the same. Beginning to sense and discover the wonder of God's world is an important milestone of childhood. Note the colors of the sunset are hinted at through the choice of red and orange in the text of the kavana.

מזמור שיר\ושמרו
Mizmor Shir/VeShamru

77

וְשָׁמְרוּ בְנֵי־יִשְׂרָאֵל אֶת־הַשַּׁבָּת ¹

לַעֲשׂוֹת אֶת־הַשַּׁבָּת ²

לְדֹרֹתָם בְּרִית עוֹלָם: ³

בֵּינִי וּבֵין בְּנֵי יִשְׂרָאֵל ⁴

אוֹת הִוא לְעֹלָם ⁵

כִּי־שֵׁשֶׁת יָמִים עָשָׂה יהוה ⁶

אֶת־הַשָּׁמַיִם וְאֶת־הָאָרֶץ ⁷

וּבַיּוֹם הַשְּׁבִיעִי שָׁבַת וַיִּנָּפַשׁ: ⁸

76

מִזְמוֹר שִׁיר לְיוֹם הַשַּׁבָּת: ¹

טוֹב לְהֹדוֹת לַיהוה ²

וּלְזַמֵּר לְשִׁמְךָ עֶלְיוֹן: ³

לְהַגִּיד בַּבֹּקֶר חַסְדֶּךָ ⁴

וֶאֱמוּנָתְךָ בַּלֵּילוֹת: ⁵

When we keep Shabbat
we are making a sign.
What do you think the sign says?

"Dancing for a מִצְוָה is when you
celebrate Hashem and the Jewish
people so much that it causes happiness
that goes straight to your feet!"

The Tefilla Text

Translation: *A psalm. A song for the Sabbath day. It is good to thank the* LORD *and sing psalms to Your name, Most High – to tell of Your loving-kindness in the morning and Your faithfulness at night.*

The children of Israel must keep the Sabbath, observing the Sabbath in every generation as an everlasting covenant. It is a sign between Me and the children of Israel for ever, for in six days the LORD *made the heavens and the earth, but on the seventh day He ceased work and refreshed Himself.*

The word אוֹת is highlighted in blue and anchored to the word "sign" in the upper *kavana*.

Educational Themes contained in the text:

- Song/music/poetry and *tefilla*/Shabbat
- Shabbat observance as a heritage linking the generations
- Shabbat observance as a declaration of faith
- Shabbat observance as *imitatio Dei* (emulating God)

The Illustration

The illustration focuses the attention of the child on the musical aspects of these two *tefillot*, and encourages reflection on the role of music in *tefilla* and on Shabbat in particular. The first *tefilla*, מזמור שיר ליום השבת, presents itself as a song for Shabbat, and speaks of singing as a form of praising Hashem. These verses are taken from *Tehillim* 92, and it is at this point in the Shabbat Evening service when those who haven't already accepted Shabbat with the lighting of Shabbat candles, accept Shabbat observance upon themselves halakhically. The second *tefila*, וישמרו, consists of verses from *Shemot* 31, and many communities have the custom to sing these verses in a beautiful melody. The theme of song and dance as a way of serving Hashem is apparent in the musical notes in the background behind a dancing Dov and Ellie as they accept Shabbat upon themselves.

The Kavanot

The Upper *Kavana: When we keep Shabbat we are making a sign. What do you think the sign says?*

This *kavana* asks the children to reflect on the declarative nature of Shabbat – what statement are we making when we accept upon ourselves the ritual and positive aspects of Shabbat observance as well as the restrictions of Shabbat? Shabbat is described as a "sign" in *Shemot* 31:17 (in the וישמרו text on the page), and this *kavana* asks the children to consider what that means. A sign makes a statement. What statement is made by Shabbat observance? The educator may wish to discuss what signs are and why we need them. Signs from the world of the child could be considered (physical examples could be used or created by the children), including signs in school, traffic signs, advertising signs, warning signs in various contexts, and so on, as a way to understand the objective of creating signs. Once it has become understood that signs are declarative in nature, the children should be asked to consider how keeping Shabbat is a sign. And what is that sign stating? Keeping Shabbat is declaring a belief that Hashem created the world, and then rested, and requires of us to do the same. It is also a declaration of faith, especially for adults, that while they could use Shabbat to earn more money, they instead choose to observe Shabbat, and have faith that Hashem will compensate them for this.

This discussion is parallel to the one suggested for the mitzva of wearing *tzitzit* (see page 16 of this Companion; pages 14–15 of the siddur). These two mitzvot could be compared and contrasted. An interesting difference worth reflecting on is that *tzitzit* is a visual reminder (of the mitzvot) to the one who wears them, as opposed to Shabbat observance which not only has an impact on the observer, but makes a statement to the rest of the world.

The Lower *Kavana: "Dancing for a* מצוה *is when you celebrate Hashem and the Jewish people so much that it causes happiness that goes straight to your feet!"*

This *kavana* is based on a saying of Rebbe Naḥman of Bratslav (as quoted in Rabbi Norman Lamm's book *The Religious Thought of Hasidim*, page 400) and asks the children to explore the feeling of dancing when serving Hashem. It is connected to the illustration of Dov and Ellie dancing, and the theme of song/music that is relevant to the text of the *tefillot* on this page. The educator may wish to use this as an opportunity to try this out practically and get the children dancing and singing. Reflecting on the experience as a group will make it all the more meaningful.

שלום עליכם
Shalom Aleikhem

בָּרְכוּנִי לְשָׁלוֹם 1
מַלְאֲכֵי הַשָּׁלוֹם, מַלְאֲכֵי עֶלְיוֹן 2
מִמֶּלֶךְ מַלְכֵי הַמְּלָכִים 3
הַקָּדוֹשׁ בָּרוּךְ הוּא. 4

צֵאתְכֶם לְשָׁלוֹם 5
מַלְאֲכֵי הַשָּׁלוֹם, מַלְאֲכֵי עֶלְיוֹן 6
מִמֶּלֶךְ מַלְכֵי הַמְּלָכִים 7
הַקָּדוֹשׁ בָּרוּךְ הוּא. 8

This special song is said when we come home from the בֵּית כְּנֶסֶת on Friday night, to welcome and say farewell to the two angels that the Rabbis tell us accompany us on the way home.

שָׁלוֹם עֲלֵיכֶם 1
מַלְאֲכֵי הַשָּׁרֵת, מַלְאֲכֵי עֶלְיוֹן 2
מִמֶּלֶךְ מַלְכֵי הַמְּלָכִים 3
הַקָּדוֹשׁ בָּרוּךְ הוּא. 4

בּוֹאֲכֶם לְשָׁלוֹם 5
מַלְאֲכֵי הַשָּׁלוֹם, מַלְאֲכֵי עֶלְיוֹן 6
מִמֶּלֶךְ מַלְכֵי הַמְּלָכִים 7
הַקָּדוֹשׁ בָּרוּךְ הוּא. 8

Close your eyes. Imagine the most peaceful picture you can. How can you make your Shabbat like this?

The Tefilla Text

Translation: *Welcome, ministering angels, angels of the Most High, from the supreme King of kings, the Holy One, blessed be He.*

Enter in peace, angels of peace, angels of the Most High, from the supreme King of kings, the Holy One, blessed be He.

Bless me with peace, angels of peace, angels of the Most High, from the supreme King of kings, the Holy One, blessed be He.

Go in peace, angels of peace, angels of the Most High, from the supreme King of kings, the Holy One, blessed be He.

The word שלום is highlighted in brown at the beginning of each stanza as is the *kavana*. The rubric on this page provides the educational background to this text, explaining the aggadic source from the Gemara (*Shabbat* 119b) that informs us this is said when we come home from the *Beit Kenesset* on Friday night, to welcome and say farewell to the two angels who accompany us on the way home.

Educational Themes contained in the text:

- Angels
- Divine Providence
- God as King of kings
- Peace

The Illustration

This illustration shows Ellie and Dov walking home from synagogue on a Friday night, and as the Talmud tells us (*Shabbat* 119b), are being accompanied by angels. When they arrive at home they will sing this song to welcome and thank the angels and ask them for their blessing and protection. The ancient *Beit Kenes-set* that appears in the misty distance and the path that leads from it to the modern street where Ellie and Dov live, represent the continuity of this *tefilla* and the long chain of tradition of our customs and rituals surrounding Shabbat observance to this day.

The Kavana

Close your eyes. Imagine the most peaceful picture you can. Is this like Shabbat for you? How can you make your Shabbat like this?

This *kavana* asks the children, using their imagination, and perhaps guided imagery exercises with the help of the educator, to experience peacefulness. Images of tranquil nature work very well to achieve this. When the children "awake" and open their eyes, the educator should ask the second question, asking the children to reflect on ways that we re-create this tranquility, and how they in particular can do that for themselves and their families on Shabbat.

קידוש 1
Kiddush 1

These פְּסוּקִים (lines 3–8) from the Torah are said in the עֲמִידָה as well as in קִדּוּשׁ on Friday night.

1. וַיְהִי־עֶרֶב וַיְהִי־בֹקֶר
2. יוֹם הַשִּׁשִּׁי:
3. וַיְכֻלּוּ הַשָּׁמַיִם וְהָאָרֶץ וְכָל־צְבָאָם:
4. וַיְכַל אֱלֹהִים בַּיּוֹם הַשְּׁבִיעִי
5. מְלַאכְתּוֹ אֲשֶׁר עָשָׂה
6. וַיִּשְׁבֹּת בַּיּוֹם הַשְּׁבִיעִי
7. מִכָּל־מְלַאכְתּוֹ אֲשֶׁר עָשָׂה:
8. וַיְבָרֶךְ אֱלֹהִים אֶת־יוֹם הַשְּׁבִיעִי
9. וַיְקַדֵּשׁ אֹתוֹ
10. כִּי בוֹ שָׁבַת מִכָּל־מְלַאכְתּוֹ
11. אֲשֶׁר־בָּרָא אֱלֹהִים, לַעֲשׂוֹת:
12. בָּרוּךְ אַתָּה יהוה
13. אֱלֹהֵינוּ מֶלֶךְ הָעוֹלָם בּוֹרֵא פְּרִי הַגָּפֶן.

What did you create this week?

What do you like to do on Shabbat?

The Tefilla Text

Translation: *And it was evening, and it was morning – the sixth day.*

Then the heavens and the earth were completed, and all their array. With the seventh day, God completed the work He had done. He ceased on the seventh day from all the work He had done. God blessed the seventh day and declared it holy, because on it He ceased from all His work He had created to do.

Blessed are You, LORD our God, King of the Universe, who creates the fruit of the vine.

The words מלאכתו אשר עשה are highlighted in olive green and anchored to the upper *kavana*; the words פרי הגפן are highlighted in burgundy, anchoring them to the wine in the bottle on the table and in the *Kiddush* cup.

Educational Themes contained in the text:

• God as Creator of the world

- The holiness of Shabbat

- The role of wine/grape juice to sanctify a mitzva

The Illustration

In this illustration we meet Ellie and Dov's father as he makes *Kiddush* for the whole family at their Shabbat table. Note the *ḥallot* under the cloth on the table, an important part of the ritual of Shabbat Evening, and a necessary presence for the making of *Kiddush*. The red wine in the *Kiddush* cup and the bottle is reflected in the red of the words פרי הגפן in the text of the tefilla on the page.

The Kavanot

The Upper *Kavana*: *What did you create this week?*

This *kavana* asks the child to reflect on their week, and what they have achieved. As the text of the *Kiddush* reminds us, Hashem created for six days and then rested on the seventh, and we are required to do the same on Shabbat. In which case, it is important for the child to realize that they can be like Hashem not just by resting and desisting from creating on Shabbat, but they can also be like Hashem by creating during the week. The educator should encourage the term "create" to be seen in its widest possible sense, and possible age-appropriate "creations" could include fun, peace, homework, a mess, happiness, laughter, as well as specific examples such as art projects etc. A child who can relate to themselves as a creator, someone who worked hard during the week, will find it easier to relate to the importance of Shabbat.

The Lower *Kavana*: *What do you like to do on Shabbat?*

This *kavana* asks the child to reflect on Shabbat as a day of positive action and experiences, rather than the all-too-common preoccupation among the young (and old) with the prohibitions of Shabbat. The verses found in *Kiddush* on this page describe the act of completion of creation that took place on the seventh day. Shabbat is a positive act that needs to be done and experienced. This *kavana* is an open question allowing the child to share their favorite Shabbat activities.

קידוש 2
Kiddush 2

Imagine the first Shabbat
after Hashem finished
creating the world…

בָּרוּךְ אַתָּה יהוה אֱלֹהֵינוּ מֶלֶךְ הָעוֹלָם

אֲשֶׁר קִדְּשָׁנוּ בְּמִצְוֹתָיו וְרָצָה בָנוּ

וְשַׁבָּת קָדְשׁוֹ בְּאַהֲבָה וּבְרָצוֹן הִנְחִילָנוּ

זִכָּרוֹן לְמַעֲשֵׂה בְרֵאשִׁית

כִּי הוּא יוֹם תְּחִלָּה לְמִקְרָאֵי קֹדֶשׁ

זֵכֶר לִיצִיאַת מִצְרָיִם

כִּי בָנוּ בָחַרְתָּ וְאוֹתָנוּ קִדַּשְׁתָּ

מִכָּל הָעַמִּים

וְשַׁבַּת קָדְשְׁךָ בְּאַהֲבָה וּבְרָצוֹן

הִנְחַלְתָּנוּ.

בָּרוּךְ אַתָּה יהוה, מְקַדֵּשׁ הַשַּׁבָּת.

Imagine the first
Shabbat after Hashem
took us out of Egypt…

The Tefilla Text

Translation: *Blessed are You,* LORD *our God, King of the Universe, who has made us holy through His commandments, who has favored us, and in love and favor gave us His holy Sabbath as a heritage, a remembrance of the work of creation. It is the first among the holy days of assembly, a remembrance of the exodus from Egypt. For You chose us and sanctified us from all the peoples, and in love and favor gave us Your holy Sabbath as a heritage. Blessed are You,* LORD, *who sanctifies the Sabbath.*

The words למעשה בראשית are highlighted in orange and anchored to the upper *kavana*, and the words ליציאת

מצרים are highlighted in green and anchored to the lower *kavana*.

Educational Themes contained in the text:

- The holiness of Shabbat
- Remembrances
- Shabbat as a remembrance of creation and the exodus
- Shabbat as a gift of love from Hashem

The Illustration

This illustration, together with both *kavanot*, directs the child to the themes of creation and the exodus from Egypt in *Kiddush*. We are still in the living room of Dov and Ellie and we can still see their Shabbat table, with their siddur open. On one page we have the illustration from the *tefilla* in *Shaḥarit*, א-לוֹהי נשמה, which is a creation scene with Adam and Eve and the animals that were created on the sixth day (page 12–13 of our siddur). On the other page we have the illustration from the blessing גאל ישראל before the *Amida* in *Shaḥarit* (pages 48–49 of our siddur), showing the Children of Israel leaving Egypt and the splitting of the Reed Sea. The educator can use this as an opportunity to ask the children why these two historical events appear in *Kiddush*. The *kavanot* may help them explore this.

The Kavanot

The Upper *Kavana*: *Imagine the first Shabbat after Hashem finished creating the world…*

This *kavana* asks the child to reflect (using their own creative imagination, and possibly aided by the teacher and an exercise in guided imagery) on what the very first Shabbat in history must have been like. The educational goal here is to contrast the activity of the six days of creation and the tranquility of the first Shabbat. This could then be connected to the child's own experience of Shabbat in their lives.

The Lower *Kavana*: *Imagine the first Shabbat after Hashem took us out of Egypt…*

This *kavana* asks the child to reflect (using their own creative imagination, and possibly aided by the teacher and an exercise in guided imagery) on what the first Shabbat must have been like for the Children of Israel, after they had left the slavery in Egypt and gained their freedom. The educational goal here is to contrast the intense activity and oppression of the slavery in Egypt, with the freedom of the first Shabbat. This could then be connected to the child's own experience of Shabbat in their lives.

א-ל אדון
El Adon

מְלֵאִים זִיו וּמְפִיקִים נֹגַהּ ₁
נָאֶה זִיוָם בְּכָל הָעוֹלָם ₂
שְׂמֵחִים בְּצֵאתָם וְשָׂשִׂים בְּבוֹאָם ₃
עוֹשִׂים בְּאֵימָה רְצוֹן קוֹנָם. ₄

פְּאֵר וְכָבוֹד נוֹתְנִים לִשְׁמוֹ ₅
צָהֳלָה וְרִנָּה לְזֵכֶר מַלְכוּתוֹ ₆
קָרָא לַשֶּׁמֶשׁ וַיִּזְרַח אוֹר ₇
רָאָה וְהִתְקִין צוּרַת הַלְּבָנָה. ₈

שֶׁבַח נוֹתְנִים לוֹ כָּל צְבָא מָרוֹם ₉
תִּפְאֶרֶת וּגְדֻלָּה, שְׂרָפִים וְאוֹפַנִּים ₁₀
וְחַיּוֹת הַקֹּדֶשׁ. ₁₁

🎵 This special song is sung on Shabbat morning.

אֵל אָדוֹן עַל כָּל הַמַּעֲשִׂים ₁
בָּרוּךְ וּמְבֹרָךְ בְּפִי כָּל נְשָׁמָה ₂
גָּדְלוֹ וְטוּבוֹ מָלֵא עוֹלָם ₃
דַּעַת וּתְבוּנָה סוֹבְבִים אוֹתוֹ. ₄

הַמִּתְגָּאֶה עַל חַיּוֹת הַקֹּדֶשׁ ₅
וְנֶהְדָּר בְּכָבוֹד עַל הַמֶּרְכָּבָה ₆
זְכוּת וּמִישׁוֹר לִפְנֵי כִסְאוֹ ₇
חֶסֶד וְרַחֲמִים לִפְנֵי כְבוֹדוֹ. ₈

טוֹבִים מְאוֹרוֹת שֶׁבָּרָא אֱלֹהֵינוּ ₉
יְצָרָם בְּדַעַת בְּבִינָה וּבְהַשְׂכֵּל ₁₀
כֹּחַ וּגְבוּרָה נָתַן בָּהֶם ₁₁
לִהְיוֹת מוֹשְׁלִים בְּקֶרֶב תֵּבֵל. ₁₂

The Tefilla Text

Translation: *God, LORD of all creation, the Blessed, is blessed by every soul. His greatness and goodness fill the world; knowledge and wisdom surround Him.*

Exalted above the holy Ḥayyot, adorned in glory on the Chariot; merit and right are before His throne, kindness and compassion before His glory.

Good are the radiant stars our God created, He formed them with knowledge, understanding and deliberation. He gave them strength and might to rule throughout the world.

Full of splendor, radiating light, beautiful is their splendor throughout the world. Glad as they go forth, joyous as they return, they fulfill with awe their Creator's will.

Glory and honor they give to His name, jubilation and song at the mention of His majesty. He called the sun into being and it shone with light. He looked and fashioned the form of the moon.

All the hosts on high give Him praise; the Seraphim, Ophanim and holy Ḥayyot ascribe glory and greatness –

Educational Themes contained in the text:

- Paragraph 1: God of creation, goodness, and wisdom
- Paragraph 2: God of righteousness, kindness and compassion
- Paragraph 3: The wisdom of nature and the universe
- Paragraph 4: The beauty of nature and the universe
- Paragraph 5: The sun and the moon testifying to God's glory and honor
- Paragraph 6: Angels

The Illustration

Due to the large amount of text in this *tefilla*, no illustration or *kavanot* were included in the spread. However, the textured background to the page suggests some of the transcendent and ethereal concepts from the *tefilla*. There is a hint of a mountain top in the clouds with the big blazing sun shining on the world. The celestial bodies, including the sun, are a recurring theme throughout the text, and this was the inspiration behind the choice of background here.

Note that the second icon of the new navigation bar, the *Kiddush* cup and *ḥallot*, has been highlighted, as we enter the section for Shabbat Day.

עמידה של יום שבת
The Amida for Shabbat Day

This is said in the עֲמִידָה for שַׁחֲרִית on Shabbat. Some of the עֲמִידָה that is said on both weekdays and Shabbat can be found on pages 50–51 and 56–63.

86

יִשְׂמַח מֹשֶׁה בְּמַתְּנַת חֶלְקוֹ

כִּי עֶבֶד נֶאֱמָן קָרָאתָ לּוֹ

כְּלִיל תִּפְאֶרֶת בְּרֹאשׁוֹ נָתַתָּ לוֹ

בְּעָמְדוֹ לְפָנֶיךָ עַל הַר סִינַי

וּשְׁנֵי לוּחוֹת אֲבָנִים הוֹרִיד בְּיָדוֹ

וְכָתוּב בָּהֶם שְׁמִירַת שַׁבָּת

וְכֵן כָּתוּב בְּתוֹרָתֶךָ

87

וְשָׁמְרוּ בְנֵי־יִשְׂרָאֵל אֶת־הַשַּׁבָּת

לַעֲשׂוֹת אֶת־הַשַּׁבָּת

לְדֹרֹתָם בְּרִית עוֹלָם:

בֵּינִי וּבֵין בְּנֵי יִשְׂרָאֵל

אוֹת הִוא לְעֹלָם

כִּי־שֵׁשֶׁת יָמִים עָשָׂה יהוה

אֶת־הַשָּׁמַיִם וְאֶת־הָאָרֶץ

וּבַיּוֹם הַשְּׁבִיעִי שָׁבַת וַיִּנָּפַשׁ:

"More than the Jews have kept Shabbat, Shabbat has kept the Jews."

The Tefilla Text

Translation: *Moses rejoiced at the gift of his portion when You called him "faithful servant." A crown of glory You placed on his head when he stood before You on Mount Sinai. He brought down in his hands two tablets of stone on which was engraved the observance of the Sabbath. So it is written in Your Torah:*

The children of Israel must keep the Sabbath, observing the Sabbath in every generation as an everlasting covenant. It is a sign between Me and the children of Israel for ever, for in six days God made the heavens and the earth, but on the seventh day He ceased work and refreshed Himself.

The words ושמרו בני ישראל את השבת are highlighted in brown and anchored to the kavana and Mount Sinai in the illustration.

Educational Themes contained in the text:

- *Torah min hashamayim*
- Moshe Rabbeinu
- *Luḥot HaBrit*
- Ten Commandments
- Shabbat observance as a heritage linking the generations
- Shabbat observance as a declaration of faith
- Shabbat observance as *imitatio Dei* (emulating God)

The Illustration

This illustration depicts Moshe receiving the Torah on Mount Sinai from Hashem. The two tablets of stone (לוחות הברית) represent the Ten Commandments, the fifth of which is the commandment to observe Shabbat. As the text specifically refers to Moshe and his role in this historical and spiritual event, Moshe appears prominently in the illustration, along with the tablets and their association with the mitzvah of Shabbat.

This is the same depiction of Mount Sinai as seen in the previous illustration on the "*VaYehi Binsoa HaAron*"

spread (pages 66–67), but this time only the summit of Mount Sinai appears. This is because the scene we are witnessing, the actual process of Moshe receiving the tablets from Hashem, was not necessarily apparent to the Children of Israel. We are glancing behind the scenes, as it were. Note again that the path to the summit where the tablets of stone await is stepped, showing easy access. The tablets themselves, or perhaps the light behind them, represent Hashem.

The Kavana

"*More than the Jews have kept Shabbat, Shabbat has kept the Jews.*"

This *kavana*, a famous quote from the early Zionist thinker Aḥad Ha'am (Asher Ginsberg) in *Al Parashat Derakhim* 51 (also quoted by Rav Waldenberg, *Tzitz Eliezer* 12:92; and a similar idea appears in the *Kuzari* 3:10) asks the children to reflect on the national impact of Shabbat observance. What impact does Shabbat

observance have on each of us as individuals, and on us as a people? Is Shabbat a good opportunity to recharge our physical and spiritual batteries? Has Shabbat observance prevented complete assimilation into the non-Jewish societies where Jews have been living for the past two thousand years? In what other ways can Shabbat be seen as important to the survival of the Jewish people?

אין כמוך
Ein Kamokha

This is said when the סֵפֶר תּוֹרָה is removed from the אֲרוֹן קֹדֶשׁ and read.

אֵין־כָּמוֹךָ בָאֱלֹהִים, אֲדֹנָי,

וְאֵין כְּמַעֲשֶׂיךָ:

מַלְכוּתְךָ מַלְכוּת כָּל־עֹלָמִים

וּמֶמְשַׁלְתְּךָ בְּכָל־דּוֹר וָדֹר:

יהוה מֶלֶךְ, יהוה מָלָךְ,

יהוה יִמְלֹךְ לְעֹלָם וָעֶד:

יהוה עֹז לְעַמּוֹ יִתֵּן

יהוה יְבָרֵךְ אֶת־עַמּוֹ בַשָּׁלוֹם:

אַב הָרַחֲמִים, הֵיטִיבָה בִרְצוֹנְךָ

אֶת־צִיּוֹן תִּבְנֶה חוֹמוֹת יְרוּשָׁלָיִם:

כִּי בְךָ לְבַד בָּטָחְנוּ, מֶלֶךְ אֵל רָם

וְנִשָּׂא, אֲדוֹן עוֹלָמִים.

וַיְהִי בִּנְסֹעַ הָאָרֹן וַיֹּאמֶר מֹשֶׁה

קוּמָה יהוה וְיָפֻצוּ אֹיְבֶיךָ וְיָנֻסוּ

מְשַׂנְאֶיךָ מִפָּנֶיךָ:

כִּי מִצִּיּוֹן תֵּצֵא תוֹרָה

וּדְבַר־יהוה מִירוּשָׁלָיִם:

בָּרוּךְ שֶׁנָּתַן תּוֹרָה לְעַמּוֹ יִשְׂרָאֵל

בִּקְדֻשָּׁתוֹ.

"Gather together the people, the men, women and children, so they will listen and learn."

The Tefilla Text

Translation: *There is none like You among the heavenly powers,* LORD, *and there are no works like Yours. Your kingdom is an eternal kingdom, and Your dominion is for all generations. The* LORD *is King, the* LORD *was King, the* LORD *shall be King for ever and all time. The* LORD *will give strength to His people; the* LORD *will bless His people with peace. Father of compassion, favor Zion with Your goodness; rebuild the walls of Jerusalem. For we trust in You alone, King, God, high and exalted, Master of worlds.*

Whenever the Ark set out, Moses would say, "Arise, LORD, *and may Your enemies be scattered. May those who hate You flee before You." For the Torah shall come forth from Zion, and the word of the* LORD *from Jerusalem. Blessed is He who in His holiness gave the Torah to His people Israel.*

The words כי מציון תצא תורה ודבר ה' מירושלם are highlighted in brown and anchored to the walls of Jerusalem in the illustration.

Educational Themes contained in the text:

- God as King of the Universe
- God transcends time
- Messianic times and a rebuilt Jerusalem
- Jerusalem as a symbol of the Jewish People as an *Am Segula* (Torah emanating from Israel today)

The Illustration

Due to the large amount of text in this *tefilla*, no overt illustration was included in the spread. However, the background to the page, a textured pattern suggesting the walls of Jerusalem, focuses educationally on the words כי מציון תצא תורה ודבר ה' מירושלם, which are highlighted in a similar color to the bricks of the walls. This encourages the children to reflect on what Jerusalem represents in relation to the words of this verse. We have explored these words and ideas previously on the "*VaYehi Binsoa HaAron*" spread (pages 66–67), as there is a crossover of verses said when removing the *Sefer Torah* from the *Aron Kodesh* on Shabbat and weekdays.

As mentioned above, Jerusalem, and all that it represents, will light the world, helping them to see through the darkness. Torah, and the People of Israel, in the Land of Israel, will bring light and wisdom to the world, through demonstrating how to live and serve God. Note in the illustration how the letters of the *alef-beit*, representing the wisdom of the Torah, are emanating from the walls of the city, and spreading out around the world. The context of this verse in the book of Isaiah is a Messianic vision for the end of days. When we as a people manage to live as a model nation, then the world will be ready for Messianic times. The educator may wish to explore the notion of being a chosen people, the concept of role modeling, and what "light" might mean to the world.

The Kavana

"Gather together the people, the men, women and children, so they will listen and learn."

This *kavana*, a paraphrased translation of *Devarim* 31:12, describes the *Hak-hel* ritual, when the king would read from the book of *Devarim* to the entire people who had gathered especially. This ritual took place every seven years on Hol HaMo'ed Sukkot after the *shemitta* year. This *kavana* asks the children to consider this unique mitzva and to compare it to the mitzva we have today to read from the Torah in synagogue on Mondays, Thursdays, Shabbat and *Hagim*. What do we think is behind these mitzvot? What impact is there on those gathered when we hear the Torah read publically? Why are those these times chosen to publically read the Torah? The educator may also wish to reflect on the verse from *Devarim* more closely – who is asked to come? What is expected from them when they are there? Is there a difference between listening and learning? Perhaps learning is an intellectual engagement in the words, but listening is more experiential, and that is what the Rabbis were trying to re-create when they mandated that we should read publically from the Torah.

מוסף של שבת
Shabbat Musaf

91

1 יִשְׂמְחוּ בְמַלְכוּתְךָ שׁוֹמְרֵי
2 שַׁבָּת וְקוֹרְאֵי עֹנֶג
3 עַם מְקַדְּשֵׁי שְׁבִיעִי
4 כֻּלָּם יִשְׂבְּעוּ וְיִתְעַנְּגוּ מִטּוּבֶךָ
5 וּבַשְּׁבִיעִי רָצִיתָ בּוֹ וְקִדַּשְׁתּוֹ
6 חֶמְדַּת יָמִים אוֹתוֹ קָרָאתָ
7 זֵכֶר לְמַעֲשֵׂה בְרֵאשִׁית.

90

This is said in the עֲמִידָה for מוּסָף on Shabbat. Some of the עֲמִידָה that is said on both weekdays and Shabbat can be found on pages 50–51 and 56–63.

1 וּבְיוֹם הַשַּׁבָּת שְׁנֵי־כְבָשִׂים
2 בְּנֵי־שָׁנָה תְּמִימִם
3 וּשְׁנֵי עֶשְׂרֹנִים סֹלֶת מִנְחָה
4 בְּלוּלָה בַשֶּׁמֶן וְנִסְכּוֹ:
5 עֹלַת שַׁבַּת בְּשַׁבַּתּוֹ
6 עַל־עֹלַת הַתָּמִיד וְנִסְכָּהּ:

In the time when we had a Temple, מוּסָף was when we gave Hashem extra animals as a gift. What gift could you give Hashem today?

"The people that make the seventh day holy will be full-up and happy from Hashem's goodness."

The Tefilla Text

Translation: *On the Sabbath day, make an offering of two lambs a year old, without blemish, together with two-tenths of an ephah of fine flour mixed with oil as a meal-offering, and its appropriate libation. This is the burnt-offering for every Sabbath, in addition to the regular daily burnt-offering and its libation."*

Those who keep the Sabbath and call it a delight shall rejoice in Your kingship. The people who sanctify the seventh day shall all be satisfied and take delight in Your goodness, for You favored the seventh day and declared it holy. You called it "most desirable of days" in remembrance of Creation.

The words וביום השבת שני כבשים are highlighted in green and anchored to the upper *kavana* (left-hand page), and the words עם מקדשי שביעי כלם ישבעו ויתענגו מטובך are highlighted in orange and anchored to the lower *kavana* (right-hand page).

Educational Themes contained in the text:

- Animal sacrifices as a form of worship of Hashem
- The Temple service

- *Tefilla* replacing Temple service
- *Oneg Shabbat*

The Illustration

This illustration hints at ancient Jerusalem, with quaint houses on rolling hills. Jerusalem and the *Beit HaMikdash* are central themes in Musaf, and rather than represent the sacrificial service in the Temple, this subtler depiction of an ancient Jerusalem is enough to explore with the children this aspect of historical Judaism and its relationship to us and our *tefilla* services.

The Kavanot

The Upper *Kavana*: *In the time when we had a Temple,* מוסף *was when we gave Hashem extra animals as a gift. What gift could you give Hashem today?*

This *kavana* asks the children to reflect on the historical sacrificial service in the Temple as a form of relationship building with Hashem. Just as when one gives a gift to a friend, leading to more love and friendship between the friends, so when we give something to Hashem we connect to Him and become closer to Him. The children should be encouraged to think beyond physical things when answering the question in the *kavana*, and should consider their time, their love, their loyalty, etc., also as gifts. Finally, this is a good opportunity to make the link between *tefilla* and *korbanot*, and allow the children to understand why the Rabbis chose to replace the Temple service with a system of prayer.

The Lower *Kavana*: *"The people that make the seventh day holy will be full-up and happy from Hashem's goodness."*

This *kavana*, a paraphrased translation of the text עם מקדשי שביעי כלם ישבעו ויתענגו מטובך, asks the child to reflect on the possible reward from observing Shabbat. The text of the *tefilla* is suggesting that those who sanctify Shabbat by observing its laws, and refraining from its prohibitions, will benefit by receiving the reward of "God's goodness." This could be interpreted spiritually, but the words ישבעו ויתענגו (they will be satisfied and take delight) lend themselves more to physical blessings from God. Those who observe Shabbat, and refrain from working to earn a living on Shabbat, are being promised here that they will not lack anything from God's blessings, and in fact will be satiated with material blessings in reward for the prime act of commitment and faith in God.

This also highlights an interesting dichotomy between the spiritual and physical nature of Shabbat. Shabbat represents a day of withdrawing from physical dominion of the world, and focusing on more spiritual matters of existence. Yet at the same time, *"Oneg Shabbat,"* requires us to enjoy the best of the physical pleasures open to us for the honor of Shabbat, such as our best clothes, food, and tableware. This blessing, that if we sanctify Shabbat, we will enjoy the physical pleasures of God's world, captures that dichotomy.

תפילה לשלום המדינה
Prayer for the State of Israel

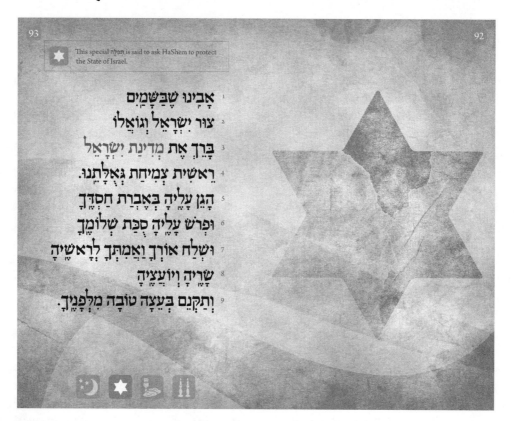

This special תְּפִלָּה is said to ask HaShem to protect the State of Israel.

1 אָבִינוּ שֶׁבַּשָּׁמַיִם
2 צוּר יִשְׂרָאֵל וְגוֹאֲלוֹ
3 בָּרֵךְ אֶת מְדִינַת יִשְׂרָאֵל
4 רֵאשִׁית צְמִיחַת גְּאֻלָּתֵנוּ.
5 הָגֵן עָלֶיהָ בְּאֶבְרַת חַסְדֶּךָ
6 וּפְרֹשׂ עָלֶיהָ סֻכַּת שְׁלוֹמֶךָ
7 וּשְׁלַח אוֹרְךָ וַאֲמִתְּךָ לְרָאשֶׁיהָ
8 שָׂרֶיהָ וְיוֹעֲצֶיהָ
9 וְתַקְּנֵם בְּעֵצָה טוֹבָה מִלְּפָנֶיךָ.

The Tefilla Text

Translation: *Heavenly Father, Israel's Rock and Redeemer, bless the State of Israel, the first flowering of our redemption. Shield it under the wings of Your loving-kindness and spread over it the Tabernacle of Your peace. Send Your light and truth to its leaders, ministers and counselors, and direct them with good counsel before You.*

The words מדינת ישראל are highlighted in blue and anchored to the illustration.

Educational Themes contained in the text:

- Love of Israel
- *Aliya*
- Israel needing protection from Hashem
- Hashem acting in history

The Illustration

This subtle illustration, almost meditative in nature, depicts an abstract flag of the State of Israel. In order not to disturb the beauty and simplicity of the feel of the spread, no *kavanot* are found on the page.

Note that the third icon of the new navigation bar, the *Magen David*, has been highlighted, signifying this special *tefilla* for the State of Israel, that can be added to any *tefilla* service.

קריאת שמע על המיטה
Bedtime Shema

The Tefilla Text

Translation: *Blessed are You, LORD our God, King of the Universe, who makes the bonds of sleep fall on my eyes, and slumber on my eyelids. May it be Your will, LORD my God and God of my fathers, that You make me lie down in peace and arise in peace. Let not my imagination, bad dreams or troubling thoughts disturb me. May my bed be flawless before You. Enlighten my eyes lest I sleep the sleep of death, for it is You who illuminates the pupil of the eye. Blessed are You, LORD, who gives light to the whole world in His glory.*

Listen, Israel: the LORD is our God, the LORD is One.

Blessed be the name of His glorious kingdom for ever and ever.

Love the LORD your God with all your heart, with all your soul, and with all your might. These words which I command you today shall be on your heart. Teach them repeatedly to your children, speaking of them when you sit at home and when you travel on the way, when you lie down and when you rise. Bind them as a sign on your hand, and they shall be an emblem between your eyes. Write them on the doorposts of your house and gates.

May the angel who rescued me from all harm, bless these boys. May they be called by my name and the names of my fathers Abraham and Isaac, and may they increase greatly on the earth.

The words שתשכיבני לשלום ותעמידני לשלום, ואל יהבלוני רעיוני וחלומות רעים והרהורים רעים are highlighted in dark brown, and anchored to the *kavana*.

Educational Themes contained in the text:

- Our soul returns to Hashem when we sleep
- Hashem can protect us from bad dreams
- The *Shema* as the ultimate statement of Jewish faith

The Illustration

We began the siddur with Ellie and Dov jumping up to greet the new day in their bedroom, and now our siddur concludes in the same bedroom, with Ellie falling asleep in a comforting nighttime scene. Note the soft light of the moon and stars, perhaps representing the gentle protection of Hashem while Ellie sleeps. Ellie's owl, a nocturnal animal perched on the edge of her bed looking over her, also intimates a protective presence throughout the night.

Note that the fourth icon of the new navigation bar, the moon and stars, has been highlighted, signifying this special *tefilla* said at bedtime before we go to sleep.

The Kavana

"Please Hashem… Let me sleep in peace and wake up in peace, and let me have no bad thoughts or dreams."

This *kavana* asks the child to connect to Hashem as their Protector, especially in the context of nighttime,

a time when all children can relate to the darkness and loneliness of the night. It is a paraphrased translation from the highlighted text of the *tefilla*.

A Guide to Using this Siddur on Shabbat

Part of the educational vision for the Koren Children's Siddur was to keep the physical siddur itself manageable for small hands. For this reason, the decision was taken not to repeat *tefillot* that are already contained in the siddur that appear in other parts of a complete siddur. For example, *Pesukei DeZimra* has not been repeated in the Shabbat section. This Shabbat guide will help the user to best utilize this siddur on Shabbat.

Erev Shabbat Minḥa

- אשרי/Ashrei – p. 35
- עמידה לחול/The weekday *Amida* – pp. 50–63 (note that the last blessing שים שלום on p. 60 is the version appropriate for *Shaḥarit* and not *Minḥa*)
- עלינו/*Aleinu* – p. 69

Shabbat Evening

- הדלקת נרות/Shabbat candles (said at home only) – p. 71
- קבלת שבת/*Kabbalat Shabbat/Ma'ariv* – pp. 72–77
- עמידה לליל שבת/*Amida* for Shabbat Ma'ariv:
- pp. 50–51
- p. 81 (taken from *Kiddush*, the words ויכלו until לעשות)
- pp. 57–63 (note that the last blessing שים שלום on p. 60 is the version appropriate for *Shaḥarit* and not *Ma'ariv*)
- עלינו/*Aleinu* – p. 69
- שלום עליכם/*Shalom Aleikhem* (said at home only) – pp. 78–79

Shabbat Morning

- השכמת הבוקר וברכות השחר/On Waking and Morning Blessings – pp. 6–31
- פסוקי דזמרה/*Pesukei DeZimra* – pp. 32–37
- א-ל אדון/*El Adon* – pp. 84–85
- אור חדש/*Or Ḥadash* – p. 39
- קריאת שמע וברכותיה/The *Shema* and Its Blessings – pp. 41–49
- עמידה ליום שבת/*Amida* for Shabbat Day:
- pp. 50–51
- pp. 86–87
- pp. 56–63
- הוצאת ספר תורה/Removing the Torah from the Ark – p. 88–89

"Build Your Own Siddur" Worksheets

The remainder of this Educator's Companion is a series of "Build Your Own Siddur" worksheets. These comprise black-and-white versions of each spread in the siddur, including the *tefillot* and navigation bar but without the illustrations or *kavanot*. They are designed to be photocopied and given to the children so that they can personalize their own siddur, using the space on the page to add their own creative commentary in the form of illustrations and/or *kavanot*, thoughts and reflections. These pages can be used as a further educational activity in the classroom, encouraging the child's creativity and ability to feel, reflect, and connect to the *tefillot* on their own terms.

The Koren Children's Siddur

BUILD MY OWN SIDDUR

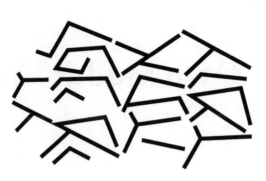

KOREN PUBLISHERS JERUSALEM

Contents

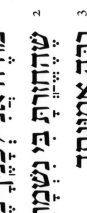 Boys say

1 מוֹדֶה אֲנִי לְפָנֶיךָ מֶלֶךְ חַי וְקַיָּם,

2 שֶׁהֶחֱזַרְתָּ בִּי נִשְׁמָתִי בְּחֶמְלָה,

3 רַבָּה אֱמוּנָתֶךָ.

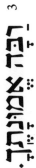 Girls say

1 מוֹדָה אֲנִי לְפָנֶיךָ מֶלֶךְ חַי וְקַיָּם,

2 שֶׁהֶחֱזַרְתָּ בִּי נִשְׁמָתִי בְּחֶמְלָה,

3 רַבָּה אֱמוּנָתֶךָ.

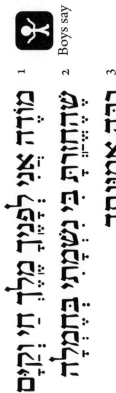

When we wake up we wash our hands in a special way.
With a cup we pour water on the whole of the right hand,
and then the left hand. This is then repeated twice more.

1 רֵאשִׁית חָכְמָה יִרְאַת ה'

2 שֵׂכֶל טוֹב לְכָל־עֹשֵׂיהֶם

3 וּתְהִלָּתוֹ עֹמֶדֶת לָעַד.

4 וְהָיָה כְּעֵץ שָׁתוּל עַל־פַּלְגֵי מָיִם.

1 בְּרוּךְ אַתָּה יהוה,

2 אֱלֹהֵינוּ מֶלֶךְ הָעוֹלָם,

3 אֲשֶׁר נָתַן לַשֶּׂכְוִי בִינָה לְהַבְחִין בֵּין יוֹם וּבֵין לָיְלָה.

4 הַמַּעֲבִיר שֵׁנָה מֵעֵינַי וּתְנוּמָה מֵעַפְעַפָּי.

5 הַנּוֹתֵן לַיָּעֵף כֹּחַ.

6 אֵלּוּ דְבָרִים שֶׁאֵין לָהֶם שִׁעוּר:

7 מָה אָהַבְתִּי תוֹרָתֶךָ כָּל הַיּוֹם הִיא שִׂיחָתִי.

8 אוֹר חָדָשׁ עַל צִיּוֹן תָּאִיר.

9 עֹשֶׂה שָׁלוֹם בִּמְרוֹמָיו הוּא יַעֲשֶׂה שָׁלוֹם עָלֵינוּ.

10 בְּרוּךְ אַתָּה יהוה,

11 הַמֶּלֶךְ הַמְהֻלָּל אֱלוֹהַּ הַתִּשְׁבָּחוֹת.

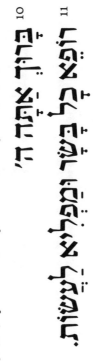

1 יִגְדַּל אֱלֹהִים חַי

2 וְיִשְׁתַּבַּח, נִמְצָא וְאֵין עֵת אֶל מְצִיאוּתוֹ.

3 אֶחָד וְאֵין יָחִיד כְּיִחוּדוֹ, נֶעְלָם וְגַם אֵין סוֹף לְאַחְדּוּתוֹ.

4 אֵין לוֹ דְּמוּת הַגּוּף וְאֵינוֹ גּוּף, לֹא נַעֲרֹךְ אֵלָיו קְדֻשָּׁתוֹ.

5 קַדְמוֹן לְכָל דָּבָר אֲשֶׁר נִבְרָא, רִאשׁוֹן וְאֵין רֵאשִׁית לְרֵאשִׁיתוֹ.

6 הִנּוֹ אֲדוֹן עוֹלָם לְכָל נוֹצָר, יוֹרֶה גְדֻלָּתוֹ וּמַלְכוּתוֹ.

7  שֶׁפַע נְבוּאָתוֹ נְתָנוֹ, אֶל אַנְשֵׁי סְגֻלָּתוֹ וְתִפְאַרְתּוֹ.

8 לֹא קָם בְּיִשְׂרָאֵל כְּמֹשֶׁה עוֹד, נָבִיא וּמַבִּיט אֶת תְּמוּנָתוֹ.

9 תּוֹרַת אֱמֶת נָתַן לְעַמּוֹ אֵל, עַל יַד נְבִיאוֹ נֶאֱמַן בֵּיתוֹ.

10 לֹא יַחֲלִיף הָאֵל וְלֹא יָמִיר דָּתוֹ, לְעוֹלָמִים לְזוּלָתוֹ.

11 צוֹפֶה וְיוֹדֵעַ סְתָרֵינוּ, מַבִּיט לְסוֹף דָּבָר בְּקַדְמָתוֹ.

12 גּוֹמֵל לְאִישׁ חֶסֶד כְּמִפְעָלוֹ, יִתֵּן לְרָשָׁע רָע כְּרִשְׁעָתוֹ.

13 יִשְׁלַח לְקֵץ הַיָּמִין מְשִׁיחֵנוּ, לִפְדּוֹת מְחַכֵּי קֵץ יְשׁוּעָתוֹ.

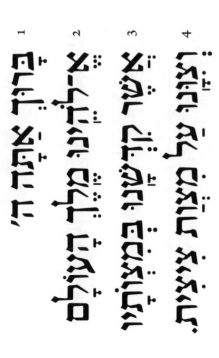

1 בָּרוּךְ אַתָּה יהוה
אֱלֹהֵינוּ

2 אֱלֹהֵי אַבְרָהָם
אֱלֹהֵי יִצְחָק וֵאלֹהֵי
יַעֲקֹב

3 הָאֵל הַגָּדוֹל
הַגִּבּוֹר וְהַנּוֹרָא

4 וְזוֹכֵר חַסְדֵי אָבוֹת
וּמֵבִיא גוֹאֵל
לִבְנֵי בְנֵיהֶם

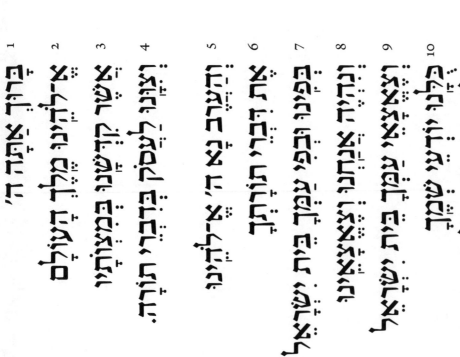

1 יִגְדַּל אֱלֹהִים חַי

2 אֶחָד וְאֵין יָחִיד כְּיִחוּדוֹ

3 אֵין לוֹ דְּמוּת הַגּוּף וְאֵינוֹ גּוּף

4 קַדְמוֹן לְכָל דָּבָר אֲשֶׁר נִבְרָא

5 הִנּוֹ אֲדוֹן עוֹלָם לְכָל נוֹצָר

6 לֹא קָם בְּיִשְׂרָאֵל כְּמֹשֶׁה עוֹד

7 תּוֹרַת אֱמֶת נָתַן לְעַמּוֹ אֵל עַל יַד נְבִיאוֹ נֶאֱמַן בֵּיתוֹ

8 לֹא יַחֲלִיף הָאֵל וְלֹא יָמִיר דָּתוֹ לְעוֹלָמִים לְזוּלָתוֹ

9 צוֹפֶה וְיוֹדֵעַ סְתָרֵינוּ מַבִּיט לְסוֹף דָּבָר בְּקַדְמָתוֹ

10 גּוֹמֵל לְאִישׁ חֶסֶד כְּמִפְעָלוֹ

11 יִשְׁלַח לְקֵץ הַיָּמִין מְשִׁיחֵנוּ

12 מֵתִים יְחַיֶּה אֵל

13 בָּרוּךְ עֲדֵי עַד שֵׁם תְּהִלָּתוֹ

1   בָּרְכִי נַפְשִׁי
אֶת־יהוה:

2   יהוה אֱלֹהַי
גָּדַלְתָּ מְּאֹד
הוֹד וְהָדָר לָבָשְׁתָּ:

3   עֹטֶה־אוֹר כַּשַּׂלְמָה
נוֹטֶה שָׁמַיִם כַּיְרִיעָה:

4   הַמְקָרֶה בַמַּיִם עֲלִיּוֹתָיו
הַשָּׂם־עָבִים רְכוּבוֹ
הַמְהַלֵּךְ עַל־כַּנְפֵי־רוּחַ:

5   בָּרְכִי נַפְשִׁי אֶת־יהוה
הַלְלוּיָהּ:

6   מָה־רַבּוּ מַעֲשֶׂיךָ יהוה
כֻּלָּם בְּחָכְמָה עָשִׂיתָ:

7   אָשִׁירָה לַיהוה בְּחַיָּי
אֲזַמְּרָה לֵאלֹהַי בְּעוֹדִי:

THE KOREN CHILDREN'S SIDDUR, COPYRIGHT © 2014, KOREN PUBLISHERS JERUSALEM LTD.

1 הַלְלוּיָהּ.

2 אוֹדֶה יהוה בְּכָל־לֵבָב, בְּסוֹד יְשָׁרִים וְעֵדָה.

3 גְּדֹלִים מַעֲשֵׂי יהוה, דְּרוּשִׁים לְכָל־חֶפְצֵיהֶם.

4 הוֹד־וְהָדָר פָּעֳלוֹ, וְצִדְקָתוֹ עֹמֶדֶת לָעַד.

5 זֵכֶר עָשָׂה לְנִפְלְאֹתָיו, חַנּוּן וְרַחוּם יהוה.

6 טֶרֶף נָתַן לִירֵאָיו, יִזְכֹּר לְעוֹלָם בְּרִיתוֹ.

7 כֹּחַ מַעֲשָׂיו הִגִּיד לְעַמּוֹ, לָתֵת לָהֶם נַחֲלַת גּוֹיִם.

8 מַעֲשֵׂי יָדָיו אֱמֶת וּמִשְׁפָּט, נֶאֱמָנִים כָּל־פִּקּוּדָיו.

9 סְמוּכִים לָעַד לְעוֹלָם, עֲשׂוּיִם בֶּאֱמֶת וְיָשָׁר.

10 פְּדוּת שָׁלַח לְעַמּוֹ.

11 צִוָּה לְעוֹלָם בְּרִיתוֹ, קָדוֹשׁ וְנוֹרָא שְׁמוֹ.

12 רֵאשִׁית חָכְמָה יִרְאַת יהוה.

עָלֵינוּ

1 עָלֵינוּ לְשַׁבֵּחַ לַאֲדוֹן הַכֹּל,

2 לָתֵת גְּדֻלָּה לְיוֹצֵר בְּרֵאשִׁית,

3 שֶׁלֹּא עָשָׂנוּ כְּגוֹיֵי הָאֲרָצוֹת, וְלֹא שָׂמָנוּ כְּמִשְׁפְּחוֹת הָאֲדָמָה,

4 שֶׁלֹּא שָׂם חֶלְקֵנוּ כָּהֶם, וְגוֹרָלֵנוּ כְּכָל הֲמוֹנָם.

5 וַאֲנַחְנוּ כּוֹרְעִים וּמִשְׁתַּחֲוִים וּמוֹדִים,

6 לִפְנֵי מֶלֶךְ מַלְכֵי הַמְּלָכִים, הַקָּדוֹשׁ בָּרוּךְ הוּא,

7 שֶׁהוּא נוֹטֶה שָׁמַיִם וְיֹסֵד אָרֶץ, וּמוֹשַׁב יְקָרוֹ בַּשָּׁמַיִם מִמַּעַל,

8 וּשְׁכִינַת עֻזּוֹ בְּגָבְהֵי מְרוֹמִים.

9 הוּא אֱלֹהֵינוּ, אֵין עוֹד. אֱמֶת מַלְכֵּנוּ, אֶפֶס זוּלָתוֹ,

10 כַּכָּתוּב בְּתוֹרָתוֹ: וְיָדַעְתָּ הַיּוֹם וַהֲשֵׁבֹתָ אֶל לְבָבֶךָ,

11 כִּי יהוה הוּא הָאֱלֹהִים בַּשָּׁמַיִם מִמַּעַל וְעַל הָאָרֶץ מִתָּחַת, אֵין עוֹד.

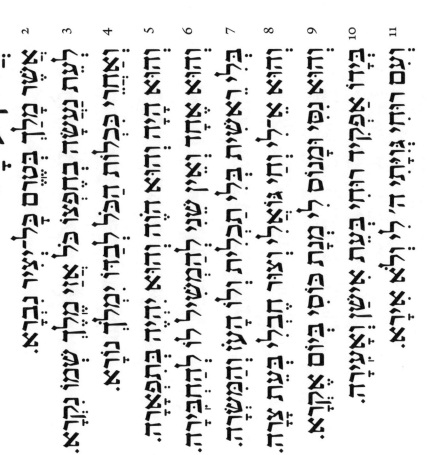

THE KOREN CHILDREN'S SIDDUR, COPYRIGHT © 2014, KOREN PUBLISHERS JERUSALEM LTD.

אֱלֹהַי

1 אֱלֹהַי,

2 נְצֹר לְשׁוֹנִי מֵרָע,

3 וּשְׂפָתַי מִדַּבֵּר מִרְמָה,

4 וְלִמְקַלְלַי נַפְשִׁי תִדֹּם,

5 וְנַפְשִׁי כֶּעָפָר לַכֹּל תִּהְיֶה.

6 פְּתַח לִבִּי בְּתוֹרָתֶךָ,

7 וּבְמִצְוֹתֶיךָ תִּרְדֹּף נַפְשִׁי.

8 וְכֹל הַחוֹשְׁבִים עָלַי רָעָה,

9 מְהֵרָה הָפֵר עֲצָתָם וְקַלְקֵל מַחֲשַׁבְתָּם.

10 עֲשֵׂה לְמַעַן שְׁמֶךָ,

11 עֲשֵׂה לְמַעַן יְמִינֶךָ, עֲשֵׂה לְמַעַן קְדֻשָּׁתֶךָ,

12 עֲשֵׂה לְמַעַן תּוֹרָתֶךָ.

13 לְמַעַן יֵחָלְצוּן יְדִידֶיךָ,

14 הוֹשִׁיעָה יְמִינְךָ וַעֲנֵנִי.

15 יִהְיוּ לְרָצוֹן אִמְרֵי פִי וְהֶגְיוֹן לִבִּי לְפָנֶיךָ,

---

1 יְיָ צוּרִי וְגֹאֲלִי.

2 עֹשֶׂה שָׁלוֹם בִּמְרוֹמָיו,

3 הוּא יַעֲשֶׂה שָׁלוֹם עָלֵינוּ,

4 וְעַל כָּל יִשְׂרָאֵל, וְאִמְרוּ אָמֵן.

5 יְהִי רָצוֹן מִלְּפָנֶיךָ,

6 יְיָ אֱלֹהֵינוּ וֵאלֹהֵי אֲבוֹתֵינוּ,

7 שֶׁיִּבָּנֶה בֵּית הַמִּקְדָּשׁ

8 בִּמְהֵרָה בְיָמֵינוּ,

9 וְתֵן חֶלְקֵנוּ בְּתוֹרָתֶךָ.

10 וְשָׁם נַעֲבָדְךָ בְּיִרְאָה,

11 כִּימֵי עוֹלָם וּכְשָׁנִים קַדְמֹנִיּוֹת.

12 וְעָרְבָה לַיְיָ מִנְחַת יְהוּדָה וִירוּשָׁלָיִם,

1 בָּרוּךְ

אַתָּה יהוה

2 אֱלֹהֵינוּ מֶלֶךְ הָעוֹלָם

3 אֲשֶׁר נָתַן לַשֶּׂכְוִי בִינָה

4 לְהַבְחִין בֵּין יוֹם וּבֵין לָיְלָה.

5 בָּרוּךְ

אַתָּה יהוה

6 אֱלֹהֵינוּ מֶלֶךְ הָעוֹלָם

7 שֶׁעָשַׂנִי יִשְׂרָאֵל.

1 בָּרוּךְ

אַתָּה יהוה

2 אֱלֹהֵינוּ מֶלֶךְ הָעוֹלָם

3 שֶׁעָשַׂנִי בֶּן חוֹרִין.

4 בָּרוּךְ

אַתָּה יהוה

5 אֱלֹהֵינוּ מֶלֶךְ הָעוֹלָם

Boys say

6 שֶׁלֹּא עָשַׂנִי אִשָּׁה.

Girls say

7 בָּרוּךְ

אַתָּה יהוה

8 אֱלֹהֵינוּ מֶלֶךְ הָעוֹלָם

9 שֶׁעָשַׂנִי כִּרְצוֹנוֹ.

1. בָּרוּךְ אַתָּה יי

2. אֱלֹהֵינוּ מֶלֶךְ הָעוֹלָם

3. בּוֹרֵא פְּרִי הָעֵץ.

4. בָּרוּךְ אַתָּה יי

5. אֱלֹהֵינוּ מֶלֶךְ הָעוֹלָם

6. בּוֹרֵא פְּרִי הָאֲדָמָה.

7. בָּרוּךְ אַתָּה יי

8. אֱלֹהֵינוּ מֶלֶךְ הָעוֹלָם

9. שֶׁהַכֹּל נִהְיֶה בִּדְבָרוֹ.

---

1. בָּרוּךְ אַתָּה יי

2. אֱלֹהֵינוּ מֶלֶךְ הָעוֹלָם

3. הַמּוֹצִיא לֶחֶם מִן הָאָרֶץ.

4. בָּרוּךְ אַתָּה יי

5. אֱלֹהֵינוּ מֶלֶךְ הָעוֹלָם

6. בּוֹרֵא מִינֵי מְזוֹנוֹת.

7. בָּרוּךְ אַתָּה יי

8. אֱלֹהֵינוּ מֶלֶךְ הָעוֹלָם

9. שֶׁעָשָׂה לִי כָּל צָרְכִּי.

1 בָּרוּךְ הוּא,
אֵל אֱלֹהֵינוּ
מֶלֶךְ הָעוֹלָם.

2 אֱלֹהֵינוּ מֶלֶךְ הָעוֹלָם, יְדֵי.

3 בָּרוּךְ הוּא,
אֱלֹהֵינוּ
מֶלֶךְ הָעוֹלָם.

4 אֱלֹהֵינוּ מֶלֶךְ הָעוֹלָם.

5 אֱלֹהֵינוּ מֶלֶךְ הָעוֹלָם.

6 בָּרוּךְ הוּא,
אֱלֹהֵינוּ
מֶלֶךְ הָעוֹלָם.

7 אֱלֹהֵינוּ מֶלֶךְ הָעוֹלָם.

8 אֱלֹהֵינוּ מֶלֶךְ הָעוֹלָם.

9 בָּרוּךְ הוּא,
אֱלֹהֵינוּ
מֶלֶךְ הָעוֹלָם.

10 אֱלֹהֵינוּ מֶלֶךְ הָעוֹלָם.

11 אֱלֹהֵינוּ מֶלֶךְ הָעוֹלָם.

12 אֱלֹהֵינוּ מֶלֶךְ הָעוֹלָם.

32

Hold the front two צִיצִיּוֹת while saying this פָּרָשָׁה and kiss them once you have finished.

שְׁמַע יִשְׂרָאֵל

1 שְׁמַע יִשְׂרָאֵל יהוה אֱלֹהֵינוּ יהוה אֶחָד׃
בָּרוּךְ שֵׁם כְּבוֹד מַלְכוּתוֹ לְעוֹלָם וָעֶד׃

2 וְאָהַבְתָּ אֵת יהוה אֱלֹהֶיךָ

3 בְּכָל לְבָבְךָ וּבְכָל נַפְשְׁךָ וּבְכָל מְאֹדֶךָ׃

4 וְהָיוּ הַדְּבָרִים הָאֵלֶּה

5 אֲשֶׁר אָנֹכִי מְצַוְּךָ הַיּוֹם עַל לְבָבֶךָ׃

6 וְשִׁנַּנְתָּם לְבָנֶיךָ וְדִבַּרְתָּ בָּם

7 בְּשִׁבְתְּךָ בְּבֵיתֶךָ וּבְלֶכְתְּךָ בַדֶּרֶךְ

8 וּבְשָׁכְבְּךָ וּבְקוּמֶךָ׃

9 וּקְשַׁרְתָּם לְאוֹת עַל יָדֶךָ וְהָיוּ לְטֹטָפֹת בֵּין עֵינֶיךָ׃

---

13 וְהָיָה אִם שָׁמֹעַ תִּשְׁמְעוּ אֶל מִצְוֹתַי אֲשֶׁר אָנֹכִי מְצַוֶּה אֶתְכֶם הַיּוֹם

12 לְאַהֲבָה אֶת יהוה אֱלֹהֵיכֶם וּלְעָבְדוֹ בְּכָל לְבַבְכֶם וּבְכָל נַפְשְׁכֶם׃

11 וְנָתַתִּי מְטַר אַרְצְכֶם בְּעִתּוֹ יוֹרֶה וּמַלְקוֹשׁ

10 וְאָסַפְתָּ דְגָנֶךָ וְתִירֹשְׁךָ וְיִצְהָרֶךָ׃

9 וְנָתַתִּי עֵשֶׂב בְּשָׂדְךָ לִבְהֶמְתֶּךָ וְאָכַלְתָּ וְשָׂבָעְתָּ׃

8 הִשָּׁמְרוּ לָכֶם פֶּן יִפְתֶּה לְבַבְכֶם

7 וְסַרְתֶּם וַעֲבַדְתֶּם אֱלֹהִים אֲחֵרִים וְהִשְׁתַּחֲוִיתֶם לָהֶם׃

6 וְחָרָה אַף יהוה בָּכֶם וְעָצַר אֶת הַשָּׁמַיִם וְלֹא יִהְיֶה מָטָר

5 וְהָאֲדָמָה לֹא תִתֵּן אֶת יְבוּלָהּ וַאֲבַדְתֶּם מְהֵרָה מֵעַל הָאָרֶץ הַטֹּבָה אֲשֶׁר יהוה נֹתֵן לָכֶם׃

4 וְשַׂמְתֶּם אֶת דְּבָרַי אֵלֶּה עַל לְבַבְכֶם וְעַל נַפְשְׁכֶם וּקְשַׁרְתֶּם אֹתָם לְאוֹת עַל יֶדְכֶם וְהָיוּ לְטוֹטָפֹת בֵּין עֵינֵיכֶם׃

3 וְלִמַּדְתֶּם אֹתָם אֶת בְּנֵיכֶם לְדַבֵּר בָּם

2 בְּשִׁבְתְּךָ בְּבֵיתֶךָ

1 וּבְלֶכְתְּךָ בַדֶּרֶךְ וּבְשָׁכְבְּךָ וּבְקוּמֶךָ׃

---

1 וּכְתַבְתָּם עַל מְזוּזוֹת בֵּיתֶךָ וּבִשְׁעָרֶיךָ׃

2 לְמַעַן יִרְבּוּ יְמֵיכֶם וִימֵי בְנֵיכֶם

1 בָּרוּךְ אַתָּה
  אֲדֹנָי אֱלֹהֵינוּ
  מֶלֶךְ הָעוֹלָם

2 אֲשֶׁר קִדְּשָׁנוּ
  בְּמִצְוֹתָיו
  וְצִוָּנוּ:

3 בָּרוּךְ אַתָּה
  יְיָ אֱלֹהֵינוּ
  מֶלֶךְ הָעוֹלָם

4 בָּרוּךְ אַתָּה
  יְיָ אֲשֶׁר
  קִדְּשָׁנוּ:

5 וְצִוָּנוּ
  עַל נְטִילַת
  יָדָיִם:

6 בָּרוּךְ אַתָּה
  יְיָ אֱלֹהֵינוּ
  מֶלֶךְ הָעוֹלָם:

1. הָרִנִי אוֹמֵר לְ

2. אֲנַחְנוּ מְבַקְשִׁים מֵעוֹלָם
   אֶת הַבּוֹרֵא אוֹר הַחֹדֶשׁ.

3. וַיֹּאמֶר אוֹר הַחֹדֶשׁ אֶת אֲשֶׁר
   אֶת הַבּוֹרֵא אֲשֶׁר לוֹ.

4. לְמַעַן סוֹבְבִים וְהַכּוֹכָבִים אֲשֶׁר
   יָצַר גָּדוֹל וְהַקָּטֹן לְכָל.

5. הַכּוֹכָב לַגָּדוֹל וְהַקָּטֹן לַיָּרֵחַ
   הַשֶּׁמֶשׁ.

6. בְּרֹאשׁוֹ

7. וְהַבְּדִיל בֵּין לַיְלָה סִם וְהַיּוֹם
   הַשֶּׁמֶשׁ.

8. הַמַּבְדִּיל לְיִשְׂרָאֵל.

9. וּמֵהַ אֶל עַל אֶרֶץ אוֹר נָתַן וְהַשֶּׁמֶשׁ.

10. וְהָרֵחַ כָּכָב לַכֹּל הַנָּתַן יָצַר.

11. בְּרוּךְ אַתָּה יְיָ.

12. יִתְבָּרַךְ הַמְּאוֹרוֹת.

12 כְּתַנֵּנוּ

11 וְהַשִּׁיבֵנוּ בְּרֹאשׁ אֱלֹהָ

10 בְּיַד אֱלֹהֵי יְ

9 אַל כֵּן נְקַוֶּה לְּךָ נָּגִילָה וְנִשְׂמְחָה בִּישׁוּעָתֶךָ

8 לְךָ תִּכְרַע כָּל־בֶּרֶךְ תִּשָּׁבַע כָּל־לָשׁוֹן

7 וְכֹל בְּנֵי בָשָׂר יִקְרְאוּ בִשְׁמֶךָ לְהַפְנוֹת אֵלֶיךָ

6 וְהָיָה יהוה

5 אָמֵן יֶאֱמַר כָּל־הָעָם וְאָמְרוּ אָמֵן

4 וְנֶאֱמַר וְהָיָה יהוה לְמֶלֶךְ עַל־כָּל־הָאָרֶץ

3 בַּיּוֹם הַהוּא יִהְיֶה יהוה אֶחָד וּשְׁמוֹ אֶחָד

2 יהוה אֱלֹהֵינוּ

1 שֶׁהַכֹּל נִהְיֶה בִּדְבָרוֹ

Cover your eyes with your right hand for the first line of the שְׁמַע. Line 4 is said in a whisper.

אֵל מֶלֶךְ נֶאֱמָן

1 שְׁמַע יִשְׂרָאֵל

2 יהוה אֱלֹהֵינוּ

3 יהוה ׀ אֶחָד:

4 בָּרוּךְ שֵׁם כְּבוֹד מַלְכוּתוֹ לְעוֹלָם וָעֶד.

5 וְאָהַבְתָּ אֵת יהוה אֱלֹהֶיךָ בְּכָל־לְבָבְךָ וּבְכָל־נַפְשְׁךָ וּבְכָל־מְאֹדֶךָ:

6 וְהָיוּ הַדְּבָרִים הָאֵלֶּה אֲשֶׁר אָנֹכִי מְצַוְּךָ הַיּוֹם עַל־לְבָבֶךָ:

7 וְשִׁנַּנְתָּם לְבָנֶיךָ וְדִבַּרְתָּ בָּם בְּשִׁבְתְּךָ בְּבֵיתֶךָ

8 וּבְלֶכְתְּךָ בַדֶּרֶךְ וּבְשָׁכְבְּךָ וּבְקוּמֶךָ:

9 וּקְשַׁרְתָּם לְאוֹת עַל־יָדֶךָ וְהָיוּ לְטֹטָפֹת בֵּין עֵינֶיךָ:

10 וּכְתַבְתָּם עַל־מְזֻזוֹת בֵּיתֶךָ וּבִשְׁעָרֶיךָ:

11 וַהֲבֵאתֶם אֶת־כָּל־הַמִּצְוָה אֲשֶׁר אָנֹכִי

12 מְצַוֶּה אֶתְכֶם הַיּוֹם לַעֲשֹׂתָהּ

1 וַיֹּאמֶר יהוה אֶל־מֹשֶׁה, עֲשֵׂה לְךָ
2 שָׂרָף, וְשִׂים אֹתוֹ עַל־נֵס, וְהָיָה
3 כָּל־הַנָּשׁוּךְ וְרָאָה אֹתוֹ וָחָי:
4 וַיַּעַשׂ מֹשֶׁה נְחַשׁ נְחֹשֶׁת, וַיְשִׂמֵהוּ
5 עַל־הַנֵּס, וְהָיָה אִם־נָשַׁךְ הַנָּחָשׁ
6 אֶת־אִישׁ, וְהִבִּיט אֶל־נְחַשׁ הַנְּחֹשֶׁת

1 וָחָי:
2 וַיִּסְעוּ מֵהָר הָהָר דֶּרֶךְ יַם־סוּף
3 לִסְבֹב אֶת־אֶרֶץ אֱדוֹם, וַתִּקְצַר
4 נֶפֶשׁ־הָעָם בַּדָּרֶךְ:
5 וַיְדַבֵּר הָעָם בֵּאלֹהִים וּבְמֹשֶׁה,
6 לָמָה הֶעֱלִיתֻנוּ מִמִּצְרַיִם לָמוּת
7 בַּמִּדְבָּר, כִּי אֵין לֶחֶם וְאֵין מַיִם,
8 וְנַפְשֵׁנוּ קָצָה בַּלֶּחֶם הַקְּלֹקֵל:
9 וַיְשַׁלַּח יהוה בָּעָם אֵת הַנְּחָשִׁים
10 הַשְּׂרָפִים, וַיְנַשְּׁכוּ אֶת־הָעָם,
11 וַיָּמָת עַם־רָב מִיִּשְׂרָאֵל:
12 וַיָּבֹא הָעָם אֶל־מֹשֶׁה וַיֹּאמְרוּ
13 חָטָאנוּ, כִּי־דִבַּרְנוּ בַיהוה וָבָךְ,
14 הִתְפַּלֵּל אֶל־יהוה וְיָסֵר מֵעָלֵינוּ
15 אֶת־הַנָּחָשׁ, וַיִּתְפַּלֵּל מֹשֶׁה
16 בְּעַד הָעָם:

שְׁמַע

1 שְׁמַע יִשְׂרָאֵל, יהוה אֱלֹהֵינוּ, יהוה אֶחָד:
בָּרוּךְ שֵׁם כְּבוֹד מַלְכוּתוֹ לְעוֹלָם וָעֶד.

2 וְאָהַבְתָּ אֵת יהוה אֱלֹהֶיךָ, בְּכָל לְבָבְךָ,
וּבְכָל נַפְשְׁךָ, וּבְכָל מְאֹדֶךָ.

3 וְהָיוּ הַדְּבָרִים הָאֵלֶּה, אֲשֶׁר אָנֹכִי
מְצַוְּךָ הַיּוֹם, עַל לְבָבֶךָ.

4 וְשִׁנַּנְתָּם לְבָנֶיךָ, וְדִבַּרְתָּ בָּם, בְּשִׁבְתְּךָ
בְּבֵיתֶךָ, וּבְלֶכְתְּךָ בַדֶּרֶךְ,

5 וּבְשָׁכְבְּךָ וּבְקוּמֶךָ. וּקְשַׁרְתָּם לְאוֹת
עַל יָדֶךָ, וְהָיוּ לְטֹטָפֹת בֵּין עֵינֶיךָ.

6 וּכְתַבְתָּם עַל מְזֻזוֹת בֵּיתֶךָ, וּבִשְׁעָרֶיךָ.

7 וַיֹּאמֶר יהוה אֶל מֹשֶׁה לֵּאמֹר. דַּבֵּר
אֶל בְּנֵי יִשְׂרָאֵל וְאָמַרְתָּ אֲלֵהֶם,

8 וְעָשׂוּ לָהֶם צִיצִת עַל כַּנְפֵי בִגְדֵיהֶם
לְדֹרֹתָם, וְנָתְנוּ עַל צִיצִת הַכָּנָף

9 פְּתִיל תְּכֵלֶת. וְהָיָה לָכֶם לְצִיצִת,
וּרְאִיתֶם אֹתוֹ וּזְכַרְתֶּם אֶת כָּל מִצְוֹת יהוה,

10 וַעֲשִׂיתֶם אֹתָם, וְלֹא תָתוּרוּ אַחֲרֵי
לְבַבְכֶם וְאַחֲרֵי עֵינֵיכֶם,

11 אֲשֶׁר אַתֶּם זֹנִים אַחֲרֵיהֶם. לְמַעַן
תִּזְכְּרוּ וַעֲשִׂיתֶם אֶת כָּל מִצְוֹתָי,

12 וִהְיִיתֶם קְדֹשִׁים לֵאלֹהֵיכֶם. אֲנִי יהוה
אֱלֹהֵיכֶם: אֱמֶת.

1 וּלְכֻלָּם אַתָּה נוֹתֵן

2 וְנוֹתְנִים רְשׁוּת

3 הַמְּשָׁרְתִים וַאֲשֶׁר מְשָׁרְתָיו

4 וְכֻלָּם פּוֹתְחִים

5 וּמַמְלִיכִים לְיוֹצְרָם, בְּנַחַת וְכֻלָּם

6 מְקַבְּלִים עֲלֵיהֶם עֹל מַלְכוּת שָׁמַיִם

7 בְּשִׂמְחָה אֶת שֵׁם

8 הָאֵל, הַמֶּלֶךְ

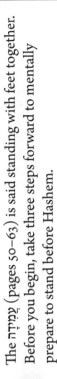

50

The עֲמִידָה (pages 50–63) is said standing with feet together. Before you begin, take three steps forward to mentally prepare to stand before Hashem.

1 ה' שְׂפָתַי תִּפְתָּח, וּפִי יַגִּיד תְּהִלָּתֶךָ.

2   בָּרוּךְ אַתָּה ה'

3 אֱלֹהֵינוּ וֵאלֹהֵי אֲבוֹתֵינוּ,

4 אֱלֹהֵי אַבְרָהָם, אֱלֹהֵי יִצְחָק, וֵאלֹהֵי יַעֲקֹב,

5 הָאֵל הַגָּדוֹל הַגִּבּוֹר וְהַנּוֹרָא,

6 גּוֹמֵל חֲסָדִים טוֹבִים, וְקוֹנֵה הַכֹּל,

7 אֵל עֶלְיוֹן,

THE KOREN CHILDREN'S SIDDUR, COPYRIGHT © 2014, KOREN PUBLISHERS JERUSALEM LTD.

---

51

1 גּוֹמֵל חֲסָדִים טוֹבִים, וְקוֹנֵה הַכֹּל,

2 וְזוֹכֵר חַסְדֵי אָבוֹת,

3 וּמֵבִיא גוֹאֵל לִבְנֵי בְנֵיהֶם

4 לְמַעַן שְׁמוֹ בְּאַהֲבָה.

These words are said between Rosh HaShana and Yom Kippur.

זָכְרֵנוּ לְחַיִּים, מֶלֶךְ חָפֵץ בַּחַיִּים, וְכָתְבֵנוּ בְּסֵפֶר הַחַיִּים, לְמַעַנְךָ אֱלֹהִים חַיִּים.

5 מֶלֶךְ עוֹזֵר וּמוֹשִׁיעַ וּמָגֵן.

6   בָּרוּךְ אַתָּה ה',

7 מָגֵן אַבְרָהָם.

1 רְפָאֵֽנוּ ה׳, וְנֵרָפֵא,

2 הוֹשִׁיעֵֽנוּ וְנִוָּשֵֽׁעָה,

3 כִּי תְהִלָּתֵֽנוּ אָֽתָּה.

4 וְהַעֲלֵה רְפוּאָה שְׁלֵמָה לְכָל מַכּוֹתֵֽינוּ.

This ברכה asks for all people that are unwell to get better. Do you know someone who is sick? Add their name in this תפילה.

יְהִי רָצוֹן מִלְּפָנֶֽיךָ ה׳ אֱלֹהַי וֵאלֹהֵי אֲבוֹתַי, שֶׁתִּשְׁלַח מְהֵרָה רְפוּאָה שְׁלֵמָה מִן הַשָּׁמַֽיִם, רְפוּאַת הַנֶּֽפֶשׁ וּרְפוּאַת הַגּוּף לַחוֹלֶה (name) בֶּן/בַּת (name of their mother) בְּתוֹךְ שְׁאָר חוֹלֵי יִשְׂרָאֵל.

---

5 כִּי אֵל מֶֽלֶךְ רוֹפֵא נֶאֱמָן וְרַחֲמָן אָֽתָּה.

6 בָּרוּךְ אַתָּה ה׳,

7 רוֹפֵא חוֹלֵי עַמּוֹ יִשְׂרָאֵל.

8 בָּרוּךְ אַתָּה ה׳, מוֹרִישׁ וּמַעֲשִׁיר,
מַשְׁפִּיל.

7 בְּרָחֲמָיו.

6 כִּי אֵל מֶלֶךְ נֶאֱמָן רַחוּם וְחַנּוּן,
וְנִפְלְאוֹת וְנֶחָמוֹת בְּכָל עֵת וּבְכָל שָׁעָה,

5 כִּי אֵל מֶלֶךְ גָּדוֹל וְקָדוֹשׁ אַתָּה.

4 וּבֵרַךְ אֶת מַעֲשֵׂינוּ וְנִשְׁמְרֵם אֶל
וְזָכֵנוּ בְרָכָה וְשָׁלוֹם מֵאַרְבַּע כַּנְפוֹת

3 הָאָרֶץ,

2 וְהָאֵר עֵינֵינוּ בְּתוֹרָתֶךָ,

1 שַׂמְּחֵנוּ וְקָרְבֵנוּ וְקַיְּמֵנוּ,

When you say the word כּוֹרְעִים, bow forward.

1 עָלֵינוּ לְשַׁבֵּחַ לַאֲדוֹן הַכֹּל,

2 לָתֵת גְּדֻלָּה לְיוֹצֵר בְּרֵאשִׁית,

3 שֶׁלֹּא עָשָׂנוּ כְּגוֹיֵי הָאֲרָצוֹת,

4 וְלֹא שָׂמָנוּ כְּמִשְׁפְּחוֹת הָאֲדָמָה.

5 שֶׁלֹּא שָׂם חֶלְקֵנוּ כָּהֶם,

6 וְגֹרָלֵנוּ כְּכָל הֲמוֹנָם.

7 וַאֲנַחְנוּ כּוֹרְעִים וּמִשְׁתַּחֲוִים וּמוֹדִים,

8 לִפְנֵי מֶלֶךְ מַלְכֵי הַמְּלָכִים,

9 הַקָּדוֹשׁ בָּרוּךְ הוּא.

10 שֶׁהוּא נוֹטֶה שָׁמַיִם וְיֹסֵד אָרֶץ,

11 וּמוֹשַׁב יְקָרוֹ בַּשָּׁמַיִם מִמַּעַל,

12 וּשְׁכִינַת עֻזּוֹ בְּגָבְהֵי מְרוֹמִים.

13 הוּא אֱלֹהֵינוּ אֵין עוֹד,

14 אֱמֶת מַלְכֵּנוּ, אֶפֶס זוּלָתוֹ,
   כַּכָּתוּב בְּתוֹרָתוֹ.

These words are said on Ḥanukka and Purim.

עַל הַנִּסִּים וְעַל הַפֻּרְקָן וְעַל הַגְּבוּרוֹת
וְעַל הַתְּשׁוּעוֹת וְעַל הַמִּלְחָמוֹת
שֶׁעָשִׂיתָ לַאֲבוֹתֵינוּ בַּיָּמִים הָהֵם בַּזְּמַן הַזֶּה.

1 וְנֶאֱמָן אַתָּה הוּא.

2 וַאֲנַחְנוּ נְבָרֵךְ יָהּ מֵעַתָּה וְעַד עוֹלָם הַלְלוּיָהּ.

These words are said between Rosh HaShana and Yom Kippur.
וּבְסֵפֶר חַיִּים בְּרָכָה וְשָׁלוֹם

3 לְךָ דוּמִיָּה תְהִלָּה

4 וּלְךָ יְשֻׁלַּם נֶדֶר.

5 וְאֶל־יְחִידָתִי מִפְּנֵי דַעַת שְׁמֶךָ.

6 כְּבוֹד מַלְכוּתֶךָ.

7 לְהוֹדִיעַ לִבְנֵי הָאָדָם גְּבוּרֹתָיו.

9 בְּסֵפֶר חַיִּים בְּרָכָה וְשָׁלוֹם וּפַרְנָסָה טוֹבָה,

8 וּנְחָתֵם לְפָנֶיךָ, אֲנַחְנוּ וְכָל עַמְּךָ יִשְׂרָאֵל,

7 וְנִכָּתֵב וְנֵחָתֵם וְנִזָּכֵר בְּסֵפֶר חַיִּים טוֹבִים וּלְשָׁלוֹם.

6 וּלְחַיִּים טוֹבִים וּלְשָׁלוֹם.

5 כִּי בְיָדְךָ נַפְשׁוֹת הַחַיִּים וְהַמֵּתִים, אֱלֹהֵינוּ,

4 בְּרוּךְ אַתָּה יְיָ, מֶלֶךְ אוֹהֵב צְדָקָה וּמִשְׁפָּט.

3 זָכְרֵנוּ לְחַיִּים, מֶלֶךְ חָפֵץ בַּחַיִּים,

2 וְכָתְבֵנוּ בְּסֵפֶר הַחַיִּים,

1 לְמַעַנְךָ אֱלֹהִים חַיִּים.

These words are said between Rosh HaShana and Yom Kippur.

אֲבִינוּ מַלְכֵּנוּ, חָדֵשׁ עָלֵינוּ שָׁנָה טוֹבָה, לְמַעַנְךָ אֱלֹהֵינוּ, וּלְמַעַן שְׁמֶךָ הַגָּדוֹל הַקָּדוֹשׁ, זָכְרֵנוּ בְּסֵפֶר חַיִּים טוֹבִים, וּכְתָב־נוּ בְּסֵפֶר הַחַיִּים.

---

1 זָכְרֵנוּ לְחַיִּים,

2 וְכָתְבֵנוּ בְּסֵפֶר הַחַיִּים,

3 בָּרוּךְ אַתָּה יְיָ,

Before we finish praying in front of Hashem, we bow to show respect, then take three steps backwards, slowly leaving Hashem's presence.

Bow toward the left as you say the following words:

עֹשֶׂה שָׁלוֹם בִּמְרוֹמָיו ¹

Bow toward the right as you say the following words:

הוּא יַעֲשֶׂה שָׁלוֹם ²

Bow forward as you say the following words:

עָלֵינוּ וְעַל כָּל יִשְׂרָאֵל ³

וְאִמְרוּ אָמֵן ⁴

This תְּפִלָּה is said on fast days and between Rosh HaShana and Yom Kippur.

1 אָבִינוּ מַלְכֵּנוּ, חָנֵּנוּ וַעֲנֵנוּ,

2 כִּי אֵין בָּנוּ מַעֲשִׂים,

3 עֲשֵׂה עִמָּנוּ צְדָקָה וָחֶסֶד

4 וְהוֹשִׁיעֵנוּ.

These verses are said on days when the סֵפֶר תּוֹרָה is taken from the אֲרוֹן קֹדֶשׁ and read.

1 וַיְהִי בִּנְסֹעַ הָאָרֹן וַיֹּאמֶר מֹשֶׁה

2 קוּמָה יהוה וְיָפֻצוּ אֹיְבֶיךָ, וְיָנֻסוּ מְשַׂנְאֶיךָ מִפָּנֶיךָ.

3 כִּי מִצִּיּוֹן תֵּצֵא תוֹרָה, וּדְבַר יהוה מִירוּשָׁלָיִם.

4 בָּרוּךְ שֶׁנָּתַן תּוֹרָה לְעַמּוֹ

5 יִשְׂרָאֵל בִּקְדֻשָּׁתוֹ.

6 בְּקִרְבֵּנוּ.

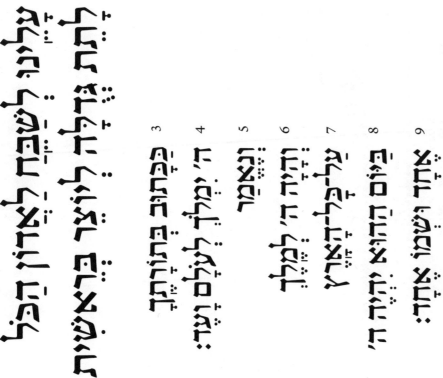

1. גַּדְּלוּ לַיהוה אִתִּי וּנְרוֹמְמָה שְׁמוֹ יַחְדָּו׃

2. כִּי לוֹ הַיָּם וְהוּא עָשָׂהוּ וְיַבֶּשֶׁת יָדָיו יָצָרוּ׃

3. הַשָּׁמַיִם מְסַפְּרִים כְּבוֹד אֵל׃

4. ה' מֶלֶךְ עוֹלָם וָעֶד׃

5. הַלְלוּיָהּ׃

6. נוֹדֶה לַה' בְּכָל לֵבָב׃

7. בָּרְכוּ אֶת ה' הַמְבֹרָךְ׃

8. טוֹב לְהֹדוֹת לַה'׃

9. אָשִׁירָה לַה' כִּי גָאֹה גָּאָה׃

On Friday night we say this בְּרָכָה before we light the Shabbat candles.

1 בָּרוּךְ אַתָּה יְיָ

2 אֱלֹהֵינוּ מֶלֶךְ הָעוֹלָם

3 אֲשֶׁר קִדְּשָׁנוּ בְּמִצְוֹתָיו וְצִוָּנוּ

4 לְהַדְלִיק נֵר שֶׁל שַׁבָּת.

 THE KOREN CHILDREN'S SIDDUR, COPYRIGHT © 2014, KOREN PUBLISHERS JERUSALEM LTD.

This special song is sung on Friday night to begin Shabbat.

1 לְכָה דוֹדִי לִקְרַאת כַּלָּה,
  פְּנֵי שַׁבָּת נְקַבְּלָה.

2 לְכָה דוֹדִי לִקְרַאת כַּלָּה,
  פְּנֵי שַׁבָּת נְקַבְּלָה.

3 שָׁמוֹר וְזָכוֹר בְּדִבּוּר אֶחָד,
  הִשְׁמִיעָנוּ אֵל הַמְיֻחָד,

4 יְיָ אֶחָד וּשְׁמוֹ אֶחָד,
  לְשֵׁם וּלְתִפְאֶרֶת וְלִתְהִלָּה.

5 לִקְרַאת שַׁבָּת לְכוּ וְנֵלְכָה,
  כִּי הִיא מְקוֹר הַבְּרָכָה,

6 מֵרֹאשׁ מִקֶּדֶם נְסוּכָה,
  סוֹף מַעֲשֶׂה בְּמַחֲשָׁבָה תְּחִלָּה.

7 לְכָה דוֹדִי לִקְרַאת כַּלָּה,
  פְּנֵי שַׁבָּת נְקַבְּלָה.

8 הִתְעוֹרְרִי הִתְעוֹרְרִי,
  כִּי בָא אוֹרֵךְ קוּמִי אוֹרִי,

9 עוּרִי עוּרִי שִׁיר דַּבֵּרִי,
  כְּבוֹד יְיָ עָלַיִךְ נִגְלָה.

10 לְכָה דוֹדִי לִקְרַאת כַּלָּה,
   פְּנֵי שַׁבָּת נְקַבְּלָה.

11 הִתְנַעֲרִי מֵעָפָר קוּמִי,
   לִבְשִׁי בִּגְדֵי תִפְאַרְתֵּךְ עַמִּי,

12 לְכָה דוֹדִי לִקְרַאת כַּלָּה,
   פְּנֵי שַׁבָּת נְקַבְּלָה.

1 הִתְקַדֵּשׁ עַל יַד אִישׁ בֶּן פַּרְצִי,
   וְנִשְׂמְחָה וְנָגִילָה.

2 לְכָה דוֹדִי לִקְרַאת כַּלָּה,
   פְּנֵי שַׁבָּת נְקַבְּלָה.

3 בּוֹאִי בְשָׁלוֹם עֲטֶרֶת בַּעְלָהּ,
   גַּם בְּשִׂמְחָה וּבְצָהֳלָה,

4 תּוֹךְ אֱמוּנֵי עַם סְגֻלָּה,
   בּוֹאִי כַלָּה בּוֹאִי כַלָּה.

5 לְכָה דוֹדִי לִקְרַאת כַּלָּה,
   פְּנֵי שַׁבָּת נְקַבְּלָה.

6 מִקְדַּשׁ מֶלֶךְ עִיר מְלוּכָה,
   קוּמִי צְאִי מִתּוֹךְ הַהֲפֵכָה,

7 רַב לָךְ שֶׁבֶת בְּעֵמֶק הַבָּכָא,
   וְהוּא יַחֲמוֹל עָלַיִךְ חֶמְלָה.

8 לֹא תֵבוֹשִׁי וְלֹא תִכָּלְמִי,
   מַה תִּשְׁתּוֹחֲחִי וּמַה תֶּהֱמִי,

9 בָּךְ יֶחֱסוּ עֲנִיֵּי עַמִּי,
   וְנִבְנְתָה עִיר עַל תִּלָּהּ.

10 לְכָה דוֹדִי לִקְרַאת כַּלָּה,
   פְּנֵי שַׁבָּת נְקַבְּלָה.

11 וְהָיוּ לִמְשִׁסָּה שֹׁאסָיִךְ,
   וְרָחֲקוּ כָּל מְבַלְּעָיִךְ,

12 יָשִׂישׂ עָלַיִךְ אֱלֹהָיִךְ,
   כִּמְשׂוֹשׂ חָתָן עַל כַּלָּה.

13 יָמִין וּשְׂמֹאל תִּפְרוֹצִי,
   וְאֶת יְיָ תַּעֲרִיצִי,

14 עַל יַד אִישׁ בֶּן פַּרְצִי,
   וְנִשְׂמְחָה וְנָגִילָה.

15 לְכָה דוֹדִי לִקְרַאת כַּלָּה,
   פְּנֵי שַׁבָּת נְקַבְּלָה.

1 הִתְעוֹרְרִי הִתְעוֹרְרִי,
2 כִּי בָא אוֹרֵךְ קוּמִי אוֹרִי.
3 עוּרִי עוּרִי שִׁיר דַּבֵּרִי,
4 כְּבוֹד יְיָ עָלַיִךְ נִגְלָה.
5 לְכָה דוֹדִי לִקְרַאת כַּלָּה, פְּנֵי שַׁבָּת נְקַבְּלָה.

THE KOREN CHILDREN'S SIDDUR, COPYRIGHT © 2014, KOREN PUBLISHERS JERUSALEM LTD.

1 לֹא תֵבוֹשִׁי וְלֹא תִכָּלְמִי,
2 מַה תִּשְׁתּוֹחֲחִי וּמַה תֶּהֱמִי,
3 בָּךְ יֶחֱסוּ עֲנִיֵּי עַמִּי,
4 וְנִבְנְתָה עִיר עַל תִּלָּהּ.
5 לְכָה דוֹדִי לִקְרַאת כַּלָּה, פְּנֵי שַׁבָּת נְקַבְּלָה.
6 יָמִין וּשְׂמֹאל תִּפְרוֹצִי,
7 וְאֶת יְיָ תַּעֲרִיצִי,
8 עַל יַד אִישׁ בֶּן פַּרְצִי,
9 וְנִשְׂמְחָה וְנָגִילָה.
10 לְכָה דוֹדִי לִקְרַאת כַּלָּה, פְּנֵי שַׁבָּת נְקַבְּלָה.

 At this point we turn to face the back of the בֵּית כְּנֶסֶת as we welcome the bride – Shabbat. Bow to greet her at the words בּוֹאִי כַלָּה and then turn to face forward.

11 בּוֹאִי בְשָׁלוֹם עֲטֶרֶת בַּעְלָהּ,
12 גַּם בְּשִׂמְחָה וּבְצָהֳלָה,
13 תּוֹךְ אֱמוּנֵי עַם סְגֻלָּה,
14 בּוֹאִי כַלָּה, בּוֹאִי כַלָּה.
15 לְכָה דוֹדִי לִקְרַאת כַּלָּה, פְּנֵי שַׁבָּת נְקַבְּלָה.

1. וַיְכֻלּוּ הַשָּׁמַיִם וְהָאָרֶץ
2. וְכָל צְבָאָם:
3. וַיְכַל אֱלֹהִים בַּיּוֹם הַשְּׁבִיעִי
4. מְלַאכְתּוֹ אֲשֶׁר עָשָׂה,
5. וַיִּשְׁבֹּת בַּיּוֹם הַשְּׁבִיעִי מִכָּל מְלַאכְתּוֹ אֲשֶׁר עָשָׂה:

1. וַיְבָרֶךְ אֱלֹהִים אֶת יוֹם הַשְּׁבִיעִי
2. וַיְקַדֵּשׁ אֹתוֹ,
3. כִּי בוֹ שָׁבַת מִכָּל מְלַאכְתּוֹ
4. אֲשֶׁר בָּרָא אֱלֹהִים לַעֲשׂוֹת:
5. בָּרוּךְ אַתָּה יהוה
6. אֱלֹהֵינוּ מֶלֶךְ הָעוֹלָם,
7. אֲשֶׁר קִדְּשָׁנוּ בְּמִצְוֹתָיו
8. וְרָצָה בָנוּ וְשַׁבַּת קָדְשׁוֹ

78

This special song is said when we come home from the בֵּית כְּנֶסֶת on Friday night, to welcome and say farewell to the two angels that the Rabbis tell us accompany us on the way home.

1 שָׁלוֹם עֲלֵיכֶם
2 מַלְאֲכֵי הַשָּׁרֵת, מַלְאֲכֵי עֶלְיוֹן,
3 מִמֶּלֶךְ מַלְכֵי הַמְּלָכִים,
4 הַקָּדוֹשׁ בָּרוּךְ הוּא.
5 בּוֹאֲכֶם לְשָׁלוֹם
6 מַלְאֲכֵי הַשָּׁלוֹם, מַלְאֲכֵי עֶלְיוֹן,
7 מִמֶּלֶךְ מַלְכֵי הַמְּלָכִים,
8 הַקָּדוֹשׁ בָּרוּךְ הוּא.

1 בָּרְכוּנִי לְשָׁלוֹם
2 מַלְאֲכֵי הַשָּׁלוֹם, מַלְאֲכֵי עֶלְיוֹן,
3 מִמֶּלֶךְ מַלְכֵי הַמְּלָכִים,
4 הַקָּדוֹשׁ בָּרוּךְ הוּא.
5 צֵאתְכֶם לְשָׁלוֹם
6 מַלְאֲכֵי הַשָּׁלוֹם, מַלְאֲכֵי עֶלְיוֹן,
7 מִמֶּלֶךְ מַלְכֵי הַמְּלָכִים,
8 הַקָּדוֹשׁ בָּרוּךְ הוּא.

These פְּסוּקִים (lines 3–8) from the Torah are said in the קִדּוּשׁ as well as in קִדּוּשׁ on Friday night.

1 וַיְהִי עֶרֶב וַיְהִי בֹקֶר

2 יוֹם הַשִּׁשִּׁי:

3 וַיְכֻלּוּ הַשָּׁמַיִם וְהָאָרֶץ וְכָל צְבָאָם:

4 וַיְכַל אֱלֹהִים בַּיּוֹם הַשְּׁבִיעִי מְלַאכְתּוֹ אֲשֶׁר עָשָׂה,

5 וַיִּשְׁבֹּת בַּיּוֹם הַשְּׁבִיעִי

6 מִכָּל מְלַאכְתּוֹ אֲשֶׁר עָשָׂה:

7 וַיְבָרֶךְ אֱלֹהִים אֶת יוֹם הַשְּׁבִיעִי

8 וַיְקַדֵּשׁ אֹתוֹ,

9 כִּי בוֹ שָׁבַת

10 מִכָּל מְלַאכְתּוֹ אֲשֶׁר בָּרָא אֱלֹהִים לַעֲשׂוֹת:

11 בָּרוּךְ אַתָּה יהוה אֱלֹהֵינוּ מֶלֶךְ הָעוֹלָם,

12 בּוֹרֵא פְּרִי הַגָּפֶן:

13 אֲשֶׁר קִדְּשָׁנוּ בְּמִצְוֹתָיו וְרָצָה בָנוּ, וְשַׁבַּת קָדְשׁוֹ

81

1. בְּיָד יְיָ אֱלֹהֵינוּ מֶלֶךְ הָעוֹלָם

2. אֲשֶׁר קִדְּשָׁנוּ בְּמִצְוֹתָיו וְצִוָּנוּ

3. וַיְכֻלּוּ הַשָּׁמַיִם וְהָאָרֶץ וְכָל צְבָאָם

4. וַיְבָרֶךְ אֱלֹהִים אֶת יוֹם הַשְּׁבִיעִי

5. כִּי בוֹ שָׁבַת מִכָּל מְלַאכְתּוֹ

6. כֵּן יִשְׂרָאֵל יָקוּמוּ

7. כִּי הֵם חַיֵּינוּ וְאֹרֶךְ יָמֵינוּ

8. עֹשֶׂה הַשָּׁלוֹם

9. וְשָׁמְרוּ זְמָן שַׁבָּת וְשַׁבָּתוֹן

10. הַמַּבְדִּיל בֵּין

11. בָּרוּךְ אַתָּה יְיָ, הַמּוֹלֵךְ הַשַּׁבָּת

This special song is sung on Shabbat morning.

12 לִהְיוֹת מוֹשְׁלִים בְּקֶרֶב תֵּבֵל.

11 כֹּחַ וּגְבוּרָה נָתַן בָּהֶם,

10 יְצָרָם בְּדַעַת בְּבִינָה וּבְהַשְׂכֵּל,

9 טוֹבִים מְאוֹרוֹת שֶׁבָּרָא אֱלֹהֵינוּ,

8 חֶסֶד וְרַחֲמִים לִפְנֵי כְבוֹדוֹ.

7 זְכוּת וּמִישׁוֹר לִפְנֵי כִסְאוֹ,

6 וְנֶהְדָּר בְּכָבוֹד עַל הַמֶּרְכָּבָה,

5 הַמִּתְגָּאֶה עַל חַיּוֹת הַקֹּדֶשׁ,

4 דַּעַת וּתְבוּנָה סוֹבְבִים אוֹתוֹ.

3 גָּדְלוֹ וְטוּבוֹ מָלֵא עוֹלָם,

2 בָּרוּךְ וּמְבֹרָךְ בְּפִי כָּל הַנְּשָׁמָה,

1 אֵל אָדוֹן עַל כָּל הַמַּעֲשִׂים,

THE KOREN CHILDREN'S SIDDUR, COPYRIGHT © 2014, KOREN PUBLISHERS JERUSALEM LTD.

11 וְחַיּוֹת הַקֹּדֶשׁ.

10 תִּפְאֶרֶת וּגְדֻלָּה שְׂרָפִים וְאוֹפַנִּים,

9 שֶׁבַח נוֹתְנִים לוֹ כָּל צְבָא מָרוֹם,

8 רָאָה וְהִתְקִין צוּרַת הַלְּבָנָה.

7 קָרָא לַשֶּׁמֶשׁ וַיִּזְרַח אוֹר,

6 צָהֳלָה וְרִנָּה לְזֵכֶר מַלְכוּתוֹ.

5 פְּאֵר וְכָבוֹד נוֹתְנִים לִשְׁמוֹ,

4 עֹשִׂים בְּאֵימָה רְצוֹן קוֹנָם.

3 שְׂמֵחִים בְּצֵאתָם וְשָׂשִׂים בְּבוֹאָם,

2 נָאֶה זִיוָם בְּכָל הָעוֹלָם,

1 מְלֵאִים זִיו וּמְפִיקִים נֹגַהּ,

86

This is said in the עֲמִידָה for שַׁחֲרִית on Shabbat.
Some of the עֲמִידָה that is said on both weekdays and
Shabbat can be found on pages 50–51 and 56–63.

1 יִשְׂמַח מֹשֶׁה בְּמַתְּנַת חֶלְקוֹ

2 כִּי עֶבֶד נֶאֱמָן קָרָאתָ לּוֹ

3 כְּלִיל תִּפְאֶרֶת בְּרֹאשׁוֹ נָתַתָּ

4 בְּעָמְדוֹ לְפָנֶיךָ עַל הַר סִינַי

5 וּשְׁנֵי לוּחֹת אֲבָנִים הוֹרִיד בְּיָדוֹ

6 וְכָתוּב בָּהֶם שְׁמִירַת שַׁבָּת

7 וְכֵן כָּתוּב בְּתוֹרָתֶךָ

1 וְשָׁמְרוּ בְנֵי־יִשְׂרָאֵל אֶת־הַשַּׁבָּת

2 לַעֲשׂוֹת אֶת־הַשַּׁבָּת

3 לְדֹרֹתָם בְּרִית עוֹלָם

4 בֵּינִי וּבֵין בְּנֵי יִשְׂרָאֵל

5 אוֹת הִיא לְעֹלָם

6 כִּי־שֵׁשֶׁת יָמִים עָשָׂה יהוה

7 אֶת־הַשָּׁמַיִם וְאֶת־הָאָרֶץ

8 וּבַיּוֹם הַשְּׁבִיעִי שָׁבַת וַיִּנָּפַשׁ

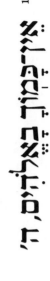

This is said when the סֵפֶר תּוֹרָה is removed
from the אֲרוֹן קֹדֶשׁ and read.

1 אַתָּה הָרְאֵתָ לָדַעַת

2 כִּי יְיָ הוּא הָאֱלֹהִים, אֵין עוֹד מִלְבַדּוֹ:

3 וַיְהִי בִּנְסֹעַ הָאָרֹן וַיֹּאמֶר מֹשֶׁה,

4 קוּמָה יְיָ וְיָפֻצוּ אֹיְבֶיךָ,

5 וְיָנֻסוּ מְשַׂנְאֶיךָ מִפָּנֶיךָ.

6 כִּי מִצִּיּוֹן תֵּצֵא תוֹרָה,

7 וּדְבַר יְיָ מִירוּשָׁלָיִם.

8 בָּרוּךְ שֶׁנָּתַן תּוֹרָה לְעַמּוֹ יִשְׂרָאֵל בִּקְדֻשָּׁתוֹ:

9 אֵין כָּמוֹךָ בָאֱלֹהִים אֲדֹנָי, וְאֵין כְּמַעֲשֶׂיךָ:

10 מַלְכוּתְךָ מַלְכוּת כָּל עֹלָמִים, וּמֶמְשַׁלְתְּךָ בְּכָל דּוֹר וָדֹר:

11 יְיָ מֶלֶךְ, יְיָ מָלָךְ,

12 יְיָ יִמְלֹךְ לְעֹלָם וָעֶד:

1 בְּרִיךְ שְׁמֵהּ דְּמָרֵא עָלְמָא,

2 בְּרִיךְ כִּתְרָךְ וְאַתְרָךְ:

3 יְהֵא רְעוּתָךְ עִם עַמָּךְ:

4 בֵּית יִשְׂרָאֵל לְעָלַם,

5 וּפֻרְקַן יְמִינָךְ אַחֲזֵי לְעַמָּךְ בְּבֵית מַקְדְּשָׁךְ,

6 וּלְאַמְטוּיֵי לָנָא מִטּוּב נְהוֹרָךְ, וּלְקַבֵּל צְלוֹתָנָא

7 בְּרַחֲמִין:

 THE KOREN CHILDREN'S SIDDUR, COPYRIGHT © 2014, KOREN PUBLISHERS JERUSALEM LTD.

This is said in the עֲמִידָה for מוּסָף on Shabbat.
Some of the עֲמִידָה that is said on both weekdays and Shabbat can be found on pages 50–51 and 56–63.

1 וְשָׁמְרוּ בְנֵי יִשְׂרָאֵל

2 אֶת הַשַּׁבָּת לַעֲשׂוֹת

3 אֶת הַשַּׁבָּת לְדֹרֹתָם בְּרִית עוֹלָם.

4 בֵּינִי וּבֵין בְּנֵי יִשְׂרָאֵל

5 אוֹת הִוא לְעֹלָם כִּי

6 שֵׁשֶׁת יָמִים עָשָׂה יְיָ אֶת הַשָּׁמַיִם וְאֶת הָאָרֶץ

---

1 יִשְׂמַח מֹשֶׁה בְּמַתְּנַת חֶלְקוֹ

2 כִּי עֶבֶד נֶאֱמָן קָרָאתָ לּוֹ.

3 כְּלִיל תִּפְאֶרֶת בְּרֹאשׁוֹ נָתַתָּ

4 בְּעָמְדוֹ לְפָנֶיךָ עַל הַר סִינַי

5 וּשְׁנֵי לוּחוֹת אֲבָנִים הוֹרִיד בְּיָדוֹ

6 וְכָתוּב בָּהֶם שְׁמִירַת שַׁבָּת

7 וְכֵן כָּתוּב בְּתוֹרָתֶךָ:

This special תְּפִלָּה is said to ask HaShem to protect the State of Israel.

1. אָבִינוּ שֶׁבַּשָּׁמַיִם

2. צוּר יִשְׂרָאֵל וְגוֹאֲלוֹ

3. בָּרֵךְ אֶת מְדִינַת יִשְׂרָאֵל

4. רֵאשִׁית צְמִיחַת גְּאֻלָּתֵנוּ.

5. הָגֵן עָלֶיהָ בְּאֶבְרַת חַסְדֶּךָ

6. וּפְרֹשׂ עָלֶיהָ סֻכַּת שְׁלוֹמֶךָ

7. וּשְׁלַח אוֹרְךָ וַאֲמִתְּךָ לְרָאשֶׁיהָ

8. שָׂרֶיהָ וְיוֹעֲצֶיהָ

9. וְתַקְּנֵם בְּעֵצָה טוֹבָה מִלְּפָנֶיךָ.

This special בְּרָכָה and the first paragraph of the שְׁמַע is said before you fall asleep at night.

1 בָּרוּךְ אַתָּה יהוה אֱלֹהֵינוּ מֶלֶךְ הָעוֹלָם,

2 הַמַּפִּיל חֶבְלֵי שֵׁנָה עַל עֵינַי,

3 וּתְנוּמָה עַל עַפְעַפָּי.

4 וִיהִי רָצוֹן מִלְּפָנֶיךָ, יהוה אֱלֹהַי וֵאלֹהֵי אֲבוֹתַי,

5 שֶׁתַּשְׁכִּיבֵנִי לְשָׁלוֹם וְתַעֲמִידֵנִי לְשָׁלוֹם,

6 וְאַל יְבַהֲלוּנִי רַעְיוֹנַי וַחֲלוֹמוֹת רָעִים וְהִרְהוּרִים רָעִים,

7 וּתְהֵא מִטָּתִי שְׁלֵמָה לְפָנֶיךָ. וְהָאֵר עֵינַי פֶּן אִישַׁן הַמָּוֶת,

8 כִּי אַתָּה הַמֵּאִיר לְאִישׁוֹן בַּת עָיִן. בָּרוּךְ אַתָּה יהוה, הַמֵּאִיר לָעוֹלָם כֻּלּוֹ בִּכְבוֹדוֹ.

Cover your eyes with your right hand for the first line of the שְׁמַע. The second line is said in a whisper.

1 שְׁמַע יִשְׂרָאֵל, יהוה אֱלֹהֵינוּ, יהוה אֶחָד.

2 בָּרוּךְ שֵׁם כְּבוֹד מַלְכוּתוֹ לְעוֹלָם וָעֶד.

3 וְאָהַבְתָּ אֵת יהוה אֱלֹהֶיךָ,

4 בְּכָל לְבָבְךָ וּבְכָל נַפְשְׁךָ וּבְכָל מְאֹדֶךָ.

5 וְהָיוּ הַדְּבָרִים הָאֵלֶּה,

6 אֲשֶׁר אָנֹכִי מְצַוְּךָ הַיּוֹם, עַל לְבָבֶךָ.

7 וְשִׁנַּנְתָּם לְבָנֶיךָ וְדִבַּרְתָּ בָּם,

8 בְּשִׁבְתְּךָ בְּבֵיתֶךָ, וּבְלֶכְתְּךָ בַדֶּרֶךְ,

9 וּבְשָׁכְבְּךָ וּבְקוּמֶךָ.

10 וּקְשַׁרְתָּם לְאוֹת עַל יָדֶךָ,

11 וְהָיוּ לְטֹטָפֹת בֵּין עֵינֶיךָ.

12 וּכְתַבְתָּם עַל מְזֻזוֹת בֵּיתֶךָ,

13 וּבִשְׁעָרֶיךָ.